## Praise for *Where the Crooked River Rises*

"As a child I loved Oregon's high desert because there was less to see, I thought, but you saw everything there was—stones, bones, weathered wood all naked in the sun…and then the closer you looked, the deeper you went. Let this book take you (perhaps shrunken as I am by life in town) far out to listen with Waterston's keen intelligence at remote Oregon places. This book accelerates the seeker's life, offering concise accounts of local character, rutted road, resonant silence, and unfolding mystery. Let Waterston locate you in dry, spare 'speaking places' where the waters of the spirit rise—'to find gold not in the easy of it, but in the hard.' Reading this fine book, you, too, will be 'burnt and instructed.' Like obsidian, emerging into a new understanding of Oregon, the desert, and human pluck, you will be 'unearthed with the run-off, and sparkle like the bright, black eyes of a newborn.'"

—Kim Stafford
author of *The Muses Among Us: Eloquent Listening
and Other Pleasures of the Writer's Craft*

"In this colorful mosaic of essays drawn from her long experience of Oregon's dry side, Ellen Waterston pictures the region and some of its inhabitants in nimble and passionate prose. Conversant with buckaroos and environmental activists, with spinster ranchers now in their graves and meth cooks taking a short cut to theirs, with boomtown Bend and tiny Paulina and nameless saged and junipered places, she confesses an "amalgamated faith" in the High Desert itself, evoking the harshnesses and bountiful graces of a storied landscape laboring to give birth to its future.

—John Daniel, author of *The Far Corner* and *Rogue River Journal*

"In this remarkable collection of essays, Ellen Waterston conjures the beauty and variety of Central Oregon's High Desert country… This collection is a treasure like the region's legendary Blue Bucket Mine."

—Craig Lesley, author of *Burning Fence*

"Ellen Waterston … writes about the "other" Oregon—the vast, sparsely populated area east of the Cascade Mountain⸱ ⸱⸱⸱⸱⸱⸱⸱⸱⸱⸱⸱⸱⸱⸱⸱ that always make me think, often make me ⸱⸱⸱⸱ head for days and weeks after I've read them.

—Guy Mayn⸱

# Where The Crooked River Rises

## A HIGH DESERT HOME

Ellen Waterston

**Oregon State University Press**
Corvallis

**Library of Congress Cataloging-in-Publication Data**

Waterston, Ellen.

 Where the Crooked River rises : a high desert home / Ellen Waterston.

  p. cm.

 ISBN 978-0-87071-592-1 (alk. paper)

 1. Waterston, Ellen. 2. Women ranchers--Oregon--High Desert --Biography. 3. Ranchers--Oregon--High Desert--Biography. 4. Ranch life--Oregon--High Desert. 5. Waterston, Ellen--Homes and haunts--Oregon--High Desert. 6. High Desert (Or.)-- Biography. 7. High Desert (Or.)--Social life and customs. 8. Natural history--Oregon--High Desert. 9. Crooked River Region (Or.)-- Biography. 10. Bend (Or.)--Biography. I. Title.

 F881.35.W38A3 2010
 979.5'83--dc22

                                                    2010030273

∞ This paper meets the requirements of ANSI/NISO Z39.48-1992 (Permanence of Paper).

First published in 2010 by Oregon State University Press
Printed in the United States of America
Second printing 2016

**Oregon State University Press**
121 The Valley Library
Corvallis OR 97331-4501
541-737-3166 • fax 541-737-3170
www.osupress.oregonstate.edu

# Dedication

To my sister and brothers Roberta, George and Sam.

And to Sambo, I wouldn't have done it without you.

# Wild Geese

You do not have to be good.
You do not have to walk on your knees
for a hundred miles through the desert, repenting.
You only have to let the soft animal of your body
    love what it loves.
Tell me about despair, yours, and I will tell you mine.
Meanwhile the world goes on.
Meanwhile the sun and the clear pebbles of rain
Are moving across the landscapes,
Over the prairies and deep trees,
The mountains and rivers.
Meanwhile the wild geese, high in the clean blue air,
Are heading home again.
Whoever you are, no matter how lonely,
The world offers itself to your imagination,
Calls to you like the wild geese, harsh and exciting—
Over and over announcing your place
in the family of things.

—Mary Oliver

# Table of Contents

# Acknowledgements

The following essays have previously appeared in the listed anthologies and publications:

"Cows Kill Salmon" in *Writing Nature*

"Day In Court" in *Oregon Quarterly*

"Last Log" in *Oregon Quarterly, Best Essays Northwest,* and *Citadel of the Spirit*

"PauMau" in *Oregon Quarterly*

"Take a River" in *Honoring Our River*; commissioned by and performed at the Cascade Festival of Music on the occasion of Bend, Oregon's centennial

"That's Deep" in *High Desert Journal*

"The Main Thing" in *High Desert Journal*

"The Old Hackleman Place: An Obituary" in *Oregon Quarterly, Connotations*

"Trapping Coyotes" in *Range Magazine*

"What One Thing" in *Oregon Quarterly*

I wish to thank the Sitka Center for Art and Ecology, the Island Institute, Caldera, Fishtrap, Oregon State University's Spring Creek Project, and the Oregon Arts Commission for giving me opportunities and support during the period many of these essays were written. Special thanks to Guy Maynard, editor of the *Oregon Quarterly,* for providing encouragement and guidance; to Oregon State University Press's Acquisitions Editor Mary Braun for her patience and support; to author and friend Kathleen Dean Moore for her inspiration and instruction; to the Blue River Writers; to Julia Kennedy Cochran, Linda Mack, Mary Heather Noble, Ruth Norman, and Helen Vandervort who have provided invaluable feedback on many of these essays and to Scott Sadil for his review and comments. And here's to fellow desert rats who helped inform this collection: Bob Boyd, Paul Cronin, Stu Garrett, Margaret Heater, Steve Lent, Brooks Ragen, and Bill Smith.

The historical references and Alice Day Pratt quotes in the essay "Two Alices" are from Brooks Ragen's study of the life and writing of Alice Day Pratt, including her many poems, two published memoirs, two unpublished novels, numerous articles for the *Atlantic Monthly* and many diaries. Oregon State University Press reissued one of her memoirs, *Homesteaders Portfolio*, in 1993.

The source of much helpful information for the essay *Morally Certain* was Edward Gray's *William "Bill" W. Brown 1855-1941: Legend of Oregon's High Desert* published by Your Town Press in 1993.

Special thanks are due to photographer and historian Loren Irving who provided the majority of exquisite photographs of the high desert for this collection, to Naida Miller for the photograph of the Pau Mau Club members, and to the Deschutes Historical Society for the use of photographs from their archives.

## Photo Credits

Loren Irving: pages 12, 15, 21, 36, 46, 92, 104, 112, 139
Michael Mathers: pages 29, 86, 115
Dave Swan: page 30
Margaret Wood: page 39
Ellen Waterston: pages 50, 94, 98, 135
Barbara Severance: page 52
Deschutes Historical Society: pages 56, 67, 117
Courtesy Don and Cameron Kerr: page 61
Greg Burkes: page 98
Loretta Slepikas: page 118

# Prologue

I RANCHED IN THE HEART OF OREGON'S OUTBACK for nearly three decades. I now live in Bend, on the shoreline of this sagebrush ocean. It's sobering and odd to realize I am a repository of considerable history—much of it anecdotal, but all of it informative about a place that is and was a privilege to experience. This high desert was an alien landscape to me, compared with the New England of my childhood, but upon first introduction I felt I had known and loved it in some previous existence. Only now do I begin to know why things happened in the order they did, to realize that nothing is a long time ago, and that I am now a part of the actual and metaphorical biota of the high desert.

My hope is these essays illustrate how the desert has "grown me," through observation of the place and those who genuinely inhabit it. This collection is a cabaret. The voice and point of view in each essay are slightly different—but taken together they offer an entertaining revue. The people, flora, and fauna of my high desert show off this blustery, hardscrabble place to be an acquired taste, a friendship that takes patience but once made, is well worth having, offering lessons well worth heeding. The high desert comes across as tough, impenetrable. But behind that toughness is a big softy, a molten heart beating not far under the barnacled surface.

I have found this Great Basin to be, at times, a harsh teacher, but it has also been compassionate, honest, loving and in love, humble, funny, straight up and forward, all the things I strive to be on any given day. The desert has watched as my adult life played out across its vast canvas—some brush strokes as vibrant as the dyes rendered from the gaudy lichens I scraped off desert rocks, some as tentative as the green gray of moist sage after a spring rain. This high desert land repeatedly reminded me that my trajectory is one among many, not to take it too seriously. To hang out somewhere between the intention and outcome, between the updraft and the down. To frame every wish as a prayer. To say thank-you more than anything else, no matter what. The sermon is not new, but the preacher, in a cassock woven of pumice and rabbitbrush and bunchgrass and volcanic rubble, is unexpected.

There is an otherness to the high desert. Something momentous and sacred in the purity of the silence. The relationship of man and nature still seems to be in appropriate proportion. So long as this balance is maintained, both seem to have an equal shot at longevity, sustainability. Through my lucky sojourn in this space, I recognize we are guests not only of this planet, but of our lives.

There are days when I subscribe to the view that we seek and then shape a philosophy to fit our experience in order to give our lives meaning, to avoid the realization that life, love and the pursuit are all absurd. The land of meaninglessness. I have spent more time in those black dog doldrums than I care to admit. But I'm now a person of amalgamated faith. Despite everything my sails are full. I have the desert lily pushing through rocky soil, the gaggle of Canada geese landing on the fog-veiled hay meadow to thank.

My years on the Oregon high desert have been blessed and challenging. My life, as I had known it and expected it to remain, was thrown and shattered against this tundra. In the process of reassembly I have created an altered mosaic, a different constellation. I now land gratefully in this place and on this page. I have come to know myself in a new and different way thanks to the lessons this grand space and its residents offer. The high desert has been and remains my touchstone and my crucible. With these essays I light my stick of sage and set about smudging my high desert home.

# Blue Bucket Gold

"EVER HEARD ABOUT THE LOST INDIAN TRIBE? The Pfhuckahwee?"
It was my husband's reply as we crested Stinking Water Pass headed
into Burns, Oregon, in 1973. He made a point of being politically
incorrect. Looking out the window of our pickup across the desolate
Harney Basin, I had asked him the ultimate existential question:
Where *are* we?

Those were no doubt the questions posed by the ill-fated, starving
families who realized too late that their cocky wagon pilot Stephen
Meeks did not, in fact, know a short cut to the Willamette Valley
through the middle of Oregon's desert. In 1845 two hundred wagons
and fifteen hundred pioneers abandoned the Oregon Trail and
followed Meeks on the infamous Meeks Cut-off. His ignorance and
arrogance cost hundreds of lives lost to exposure and dehydration.

Perhaps the ghosts of those who died on that expedition would
have had something to tell me about heading out into this desert,
had I known to ask, would have had something to tell me about
paying attention, taking stock and responsibility, learning as much
as possible about an idea, a dream before pursuing it, not acting on

fantasy. But I was young and so was my husband. His felt cowboy hat perched jauntily on his head. He knew the language and cadence of the land, of livestock. He was fluent in *lepy* and *cavvy*, *picking string*, *gant* and *snuffy*, spoke fescue, needle and thread, crested wheat and bunchgrass. We were brave and uninformed, mostly about ourselves and each other.

And we were in love. In our rundown pickup with Montana plates and cab-over camper we looked more like evacuees from the Dust Bowl than qualified ranch buyers. Entering from the Burns end of things my first introduction to Oregon was the unrelenting straight-arrow of Highway 20 across Harney Valley, the alkaline flats with whorls of geese, egret, crane lifting like apparitions; waterlogged, lifeless tree-skeletons stranded in alkaline flats; and in the distance, the landlocked Malheur Lake. As we ventured farther into the bleak rabbitbrush and bunchgrass tundra of the high desert, my husband spat into the brass spittoon balanced on the transom between the pickup seats and remarked: "Around here a cow's gonna have to eat at a trot just to survive. Gonna need a square mile per head. That's on a good year." Coming from the overly generous grasslands of eastern Montana we found this pocked, arid land uneasy, unhealthy, uninviting. But with coal development displacing ranchers and putting our coal-less, grass-rich Montana ranch at a premium, it was time to sell and go.

Why Oregon? We were young enough to still think a whim was a factual survey. A Montana rancher friend had mentioned something about the lush John Day valley so we thought we'd check it out, felt confident we'd find our version of gold.

For truck drivers Highway 20 between Burns and Bend is a stretch that requires extra coffee to counter the effects of the tick-ticking of the center line, the hypnotic dance of the phone wires. The only distractions are the Brothers and Hampton stores, open when the spirit grabs. Or the Millican store, now boarded up, the whole town, including the skeletons of barns, corrals, and houses, for sale. This was a novelty to me. Where I came from in New England, houses weren't left to die, left to the forces of nature, the paint-peeling heat, persistent wind licking up the edges of shingles, weeds worrying the porch boards up and away from their ten-penny nails. Here windmills slumped like collapsed giraffes on the horizon, the wooden frame that once held them up now dismantled by the elements. This high desert, it seemed, wasn't much impressed by man's monuments to himself, tended to take itself back.

Most want to rush through this desert stretch on their way to Sun Valley or Boise or Bend or Portland, as though the parched isolation and loneliness are catching. As though it reminds them of their mortality and "no, thank you." As though the space could snatch them up and sentence them to a life in this remote, windswept barren land. What passersby don't see, and neither did I on that first disheartening introduction, is the sagebrush prayerfully folding up its leaves in the heat of the day to retain moisture and then at night opening its tiny gray-green palms to receive the dew. What they don't see is the tuft of deer hair on the barbed-wire fence, the wild gooseberry, the blush of green on the face of a rimrock where a small spring emerges. They don't see the vast expanses where the pronghorn run so crazy they seem caught in an energy vortex. A place where, as Oregon poet William Stafford said, "the least little sound sets the coyotes walking." What they don't see, forty miles off the highway at Hampton, is where the South Fork of the Crooked River magically rises, stilt-legged shore birds and red-winged blackbirds decorating this spontaneous combustion of water amidst wagging cattails and shivering willows. It offers itself up, unassuming and staggeringly beautiful, at what is now the headquarters of the GI Ranch, one of Oregon's oldest.

The Meeks party is said to have traversed the Malheur Mountains and then the endless flat of Harney Valley, more or less the stretch of land that Highway 20 traverses. Desperate for a source of potable water, they pushed on. Traces of encampments—initials carved in the bark of juniper trees, fossilized wagon tracks, old graves—are said to have been found along the Little Malheur, at Crane and Trout creeks, at Buck Creek, and then finally at the headwaters of the Crooked

River, which offered an abundance of what they were desperate for: water.

Prophetically, our traverse across eastern Oregon wasn't all that different than that of the ill-fated Meeks group. Instead of coming in through John Day we got turned around and, like the wagon train, came in through Harney Valley, Ontario, Vale, Burns, Hampton, Brothers, Millican. We eventually made our way to the Deschutes River and Bend and to the realty office of Farris Spaulding. He had managed the GI Ranch for years and knew of a neighboring place that was for sale. We ended up buying it, what was then known as the old Hackleman Place, the next ranch down from the GI, the next one down from where the Crooked River spills like liquid gold out of the earth.

Speaking of gold: some claim that river-rise is where the legendary Blue Bucket Mine is located. The story is that a member, some say a child, of the Meeks party found shiny nuggets in the water and carried them back to the wagon train in a blue bucket. Buckets were made of wood in those days and painted to protect and preserve the wood. According to accounts, the Meeks party was so intent on survival that the pliable material was fashioned into weights for fishing lines and other utilitarian purposes. It is speculated that before the weary travelers realized the soft metal was the mother lode, the wagon train had labored its way from the Deschutes River to The Dalles and then down the Columbia on rafts to the Willamette Valley. By that time they were too far gone to return and accounts of where the gold had been found were obscured by the miles that separated them from that desert oasis.

What were they looking for? What were *we* looking for? A place to settle? Call home? A new beginning? An escape from a situation or culture? At what point did they (or do any of us) realize they were off course? At that point what were the options? Isn't it true that as we fly off into the space of our lives, the weightless distance between the better decision and the wrong one becomes greater and greater, the ability to return to claim what turns out to have been the real gold becomes less feasible, then impossible—and finally the wrong decision becomes our life story, leaving us no choice but to live into it?

In the face of the tragic and unhappy endings I experienced—my marriage, shared dreams of ranching, my former husband's drug-induced suicide—so much of what initially filled my blue bucket has been tainted by experience and time. The powerful sense of homecoming I felt when we first laid eyes on our ranch-to-be nestled in the steep valley of the South Fork is now shrouded. Dreamlike now are recollections of spring calves, hardworking dogs, smart horses, trim, tall stacks of alfalfa, the hammock suspended between two big cottonwoods that shaded the ranch house we refurbished, the demitasse sets and silverware—wedding presents from fellow New Englanders ignorant of the life we had embarked on. (In the excavation of roads for tiny trucks and the shaping of mud pies many of the silver teaspoons were lost in the children's sandbox. One day, perhaps, there will be rumors of the Sandbox Silver Mine.) For me the task has been to find gold not in the easy of it, but in the hard. How has the failure of what I placed stock in revealed me to myself? How has what was lost become my guide? It turns out the violent volcanoes and earthquakes of my experience, the deep magma pools of unsolvable sadness, are where gold-filled veins of quartz, the philosopher's stone are lodged.

Aren't all of us on a search for the Blue Bucket Mine of our imagination—the perfect relationship, place, profession, loving children, health, happiness? The pure ore, the standard-bearer, what we all aspire to be or experience in our lives? I am. I ferret about, keep, discard, dig deeper here, skim the surface there, carve ambitions into the bark of this or that juniper tree, leave behind fossilized wagon tracks that document my zigs and zags.

When life seems to mete uneven portions of luck, intuition, and wisdom, and the alchemy of miracle, magic, and good fortune remain elusive, I go back, retrace my steps, pan the same material over and over, looking for the glitter, the real gold, that store of promise somehow missed, passed by and now a repository for regret.

This constant panning only serves to keep the waters perpetually murky, makes it impossible to see clearly what sprite opportunity lies on the bottom or floats within reach. The constant panning misses the point. Just what is the gold standard I hold myself up to? According to whom? Only the fool values a gold that can only look, feel, bend a certain way. In the end all that glitters is the real thing. Because what each of us experiences as gold makes it so. The light of our attention and love makes it so. It sounds so simple.

# Rock Hound

"SO, YOU DECIDED TO JOIN THE RANKS of desert rats and rock hounds?" a neighbor inquired of me at a branding soon after our arrival at our desert ranch. The desert rat moniker I knew about. My husband and I had joined the chorus of those who cursed the Townsend Ground Squirrel, the unwelcome rodent that burrowed holes in hay fields and irrigation ditches. We joined in offering our population of sage rats for target practice to hunters who'd swarm the ranch in spring. But a rock hound? Those words, the unnatural juxtaposition of images—whatever the meaning, I didn't want to be associated with such a term, never mind *be* one.

Early in his marriage, a close friend of my parents left Boston and took his bride to Ellensburg, Washington, to try ranching on for size. He ultimately succumbed to familial and cultural pressure, returning to Harvard law school and a career at a fancy firm. Now in his eighties, his idea of adventure has been reduced to his weekly ROMEO (retired old men eating out) meeting in downtown Boston. But when he was younger his abiding love of the ranching West prompted him to visit our ranch more than once.

"You lucky girl! You live in the rock hound capital of the United States," he announced to me when I met him at the Redmond airport on the occasion of his first trip. He might as well have uttered an obscenity, so odd was it to hear such a word come from him, a proper New Englander and all.

"You know about rock hounds?" I asked incredulously.

"Yes, I am one."

I learned from him that I had unknowingly moved to a land of petrified wood, limb casts, moss agate, red and yellow jasper, copper-colored sunstone, obsidian—brilliant constructs of molten magma. Compressed, crystallized, pulverized, scorched, shattered perfections birthed from volcanic upheaval and chaos millions of years ago had worked their way to the surface, worked their way onto the pale, smooth throats and soft earlobes of decorated women, onto the blunt ring fingers of men. I had moved to a state whose official rock was the thunder egg. To a place where people designed vacations around Petersen's Rock Garden, rock hound powwows, Richardson Rock Ranch, or the Spectrum Sunstone Mine, swerved off the road to stop and check out rock shops. One of my local favorites is designated by an enormous boulder nesting on the crushed roof of a garishly painted car in front of a straight-talking sign: Rocks.

A rock hound is a hobby geologist, one who collects and studies rocks and minerals. And they do it in the most remote places, on their hands and knees, scratching, chipping, digging. They are armed with hammers, chisels, plastic bags, hand lenses, penknives, streak plates, magnets, and, yes, old dental tools. Rock hound festivals are held throughout this part of the West, rock carnies tending collapsible aluminum tables laden with, well, rocks. Prineville's festival is held each June, followed by festivals in Redmond and Sisters. "Festival" suggests noise and gaiety. That's not the prevailing ambiance at a rock hound festival or "powwow," as they are commonly called, unless the clackety-clack of rock tumblers counts. More likely there's an assortment of RVs parked on the festival grounds, portable lawn chairs with coffee-toting beverage holders in the armrests set up alongside. There is a sense of time unlimited as people from all over the world meander through the maze of tables that strain under dusty wooden bins and Tupperware containers filled with what ninety percent of the population would never notice or remark on. But these rockhounders pick up and, with respect and awe, turn the stones and polished gems thoughtfully, look at them appreciatively, consider their violent history and the resolution of that journey into something they deem truly beautiful.

From what I have gleaned, the Great Basin region was twice submerged under water—first salt, unimaginably long ago (try 380 million years), and then fresh. As the fresh water receded during the Eocene, when the Clarno volcanoes created an arc of fireworks from northeastern Oregon to Prineville, exotic mammals wandered the shores of lakes, feasted on lush vegetation—wooly mammoths, three-toed horses, strange camels, and the tapir. Then came the Ice Age of the Pleistocene, 1.8 million years ago. During this time Steens Mountain boasted glaciers; Summer and Abert lakes were one big body of water. Glacier dams in the Clark Fork River in Idaho formed the infamous Missoula Lake which, at the end of that epoch, "only" eight thousand years ago, gave way, setting off one of the great floods of all time, scouring the Columbia River Gorge and turning the Willamette Valley into a lake. About this time the volcanic fireworks that formed the Cascades claimed the stage. Those peaks ultimately blocked precipitation, and the region that would become the high desert had to adapt to being a land of little rain, an annual average of about twelve inches.

Just as a thin, gossamer ring of breathable air supports human life on earth, the habitable surface of the earth floats on a hot magma porridge. Some of the great scarps of the high desert, such as Warner Valley and Hart Mountain, are impressively close to the hot interior of earth as little as four miles separating the surface from the molten stew. Combine the hot air of that mantle with a freshwater source and the hot springs that delight people at Juntura, Crane, Hart Mountain, and Izee are formed. The hot magma is always seeking a pathway to pitch a fit, boil up and through. The South Sister, with the growing bulge on its south flank, is currently contemplating just such a tantrum. But it is this dynamic and dramatic crucible of salt to fresh to volcanic crush to massive flows of ice that created the extraordinary fossil formations and exotic rocks that the rock hound finds so compelling.

Initially my rockhounding was, out of my ignorance of the area's spectacular geology, limited to hunting for obsidian arrowheads in the spring. We had a sometime ranch hand who was part Native American and taught me where to look, what to look for. Our ranch was northeast of a well-known source of prized obsidian—Glass Butte, which erupted a mere 4.9 million years ago. So keen and in demand was this fire-glass for making arrowheads and knives, obsidian from this large land formation was found traded by Indians all the way to Mississippi and beyond. The very words used to describe obsidian, which is formed by the rapid cooling of magma, sound hot and mysterious: chatoyant, iridescent, aventurescent. Fire, flame, and rainbow obsidian are all found on Glass Butte, as are the mahogany, gold, and sheen varieties. In the draws and coulees around the ranch the runoff each spring would uncover fists of the black glass as well as chips and, in many cases, perfect arrowheads, spears, and other tools made of obsidian.

After putting my children down for their afternoon nap, I would head up one of the steep bluffs within view of the ranch house, my blue heeler trailing along behind, to hunt for the telltale black glinting through the gritty desert soil. Seeing something, I'd work the dirt away with my toe, then bend over, pick up the piece, study it for signs of having been worked by other hands, shining it on the back of my jeans to get a better look. Sometimes I'd also come across teepee rings or fire circles on those hilltops, or signs of later inhabitants of the desert, herders and buckaroos, who whiled away their time building cairns as directional markers or a random run of wall out of volcanic

tuff to deflect sheep or cattle one way or another—the wall pitching
headlong down the face of a hill, starting at nothing that felt like a
beginning, stopping at nothing that felt like an end.

Some New Agers say obsidian protects, grounds, removes
negativity while also causing rapid change and learning. I didn't know
that then, but in hindsight I'd have to agree. I feel both burnt and
instructed, tumbled and protected by my time in this desert. Seated
inside a fire circle on the slope of that bluff, in the middle of that vast
nowhere, what a miniscule punctuation mark my existence made as,
unbeknownst to me, its engines were being fired by the latent heat
and metaphorical, maybe even metaphysical, power of obsidian.
I basked in the sun-baked silence, my dog curled gratefully in my
shadow. In the house below my children slept, on the kitchen counter
meat lay out to thaw for that night's dinner, by my feet desert lily and
bitterroot bloomed.

When my youngest was four I was accepted into a writing
workshop led by Ursula LeGuin. My poems and essays were being
published here and there, but this was the first time I had ever
attended such a retreat. We stayed in old Quonset huts at the Malheur
Field Station in Harney County, ate in the communal kitchen along
with Elder Hostel groups on birding expeditions and earnest graduate
students studying the environs of landlocked Harney Lake. Ursula
LeGuin is inspirational as a writer, as an activist, as a person. And
she loves the high desert. In her wonderful, wry, brave, imaginative,
and mischievous way she seems a cousin to the coyote. She shared
that some of the fantastical landscapes in her writing were inspired
by favorite places in and around Steens Mountain and the Malheur
National Wildlife Refuge.

As is typical of this sort of gathering of writers, we were a random
group of people with little in common other than an interest in
improving our craft. Or so we thought. It turned out that each of
us had serendipitously stumbled on this opportunity to receive not
only Ursula LeGuin's teaching but also the teachings of this magical
part of the world. Maybe those were obsidian chips on our morning

cereal. Everything about our time there seemed an altered reality, something conjured by Carlos Castaneda—from the magpie that befriended me, hopping onto my desk to deposit bits of sun-bleached tire tread or shiny bits of mica; to all of us leaping naked into the unplumbed calderas of small volcanoes, our bodies piercing the slime-coated surface and disappearing into the magma-heated water; to lying spread-eagle on our backs at night on the bristly ground, coyotes howling all around, as we stared up at the Milky Way, a gauze curtain pulled across eternity.

On one afternoon field trip we were taken to a nondescript location where there were said to be thunder eggs, "geode-like bodies of chalcedon, opal or agate weathered out of welded tuffs," the pamphlet explained. "The result of trapped pockets of gas as molten rocks cooled." One less-than-scientific explanation is that thunder eggs were made by surviving at least two volcanic eruptions, the second blast coating and cooking the first—forming crystalline caverns inside the newly minted shell—often with loose particles of crystal that rattle when you shake the rock. The name is said to derive from a Native American legend in which the gods of Mt. Hood and Mt. Jefferson threw thunderbolts at one another, and the thunder eggs were the result of these quarrels. We crawled around like insane people, picking up nondescript round, brown rocks and shaking them vigorously next to our ears. I found three thunder eggs, or lava core bombs, as they are also called, one for each of my children, each with a different song sealed tightly inside.

For the participants in Ursula's workshop the thunder egg was a fitting symbol. The retreat turned out to be the opportunity to honor being thunder-egged by our lives, and taking the time to listen for, reflect on, and write about the fragile, glassy symphony that played inside us and those we loved, a symphony made of the beauty of brokenness.

The week turned most of us completely upside down, prompted us to jettison careers, marriages, recommit or commit to writing. As for me, it fueled a sense of who I was separate from my marriage, from my husband's debilitating addictions, and confirmed my desert rat status. It would be only weeks after the retreat that I gathered up my children, their clutch of thunder eggs, and left the ranch I loved.

A few years later—cobbling together a livelihood, managing and not managing the challenges of single parenting—I drove with a friend out of Bend east toward the desert to walk along a dry riverbed. It was formed by ash from Mt. Mazama, deposited seventy-seven hundred years ago, the same time Crater Lake was formed. The monumental rocks along this bed were smoothed by an ancient river that drained Lake Millican during a lull in the Ice Age. Many Native Americans used the smooth faces of the boulders to inscribe urgent, shaman-like figures with sun circles radiating out from their heads or energetic deer figures, cartwheeling stick figures. It was dusk when we arrived, the silhouettes of the gray-green juniper trees visible along the path. We walked in silence in deference to the sacredness of place we felt while walking toward the head of the canyon. I happened to glance over at a juniper as we passed and there, cupped in the palm of a branch that extended toward me, was a crystal. It was as though it grew there, as though the fruit of this tree. I accepted the gift, felt catapulted to Earth's very center by the mystery and magic of this happenstance.

Crystals too are ascribed meanings and powers. Stare at a crystal and it stares boldly back. Harder than steel, they are in fact eons frozen in time. They allow us to peer through their incredible density with the naked eye. The one handed to me by the juniper tree was what is referred to as an "Empathetic Warrior," characterized by cloudiness, nicks, and chips. It is said to help one through challenge or injury, to teach appreciation of the beauty within oneself, to facilitate communication with nature and spirit. By now I was onto these rock angels, and paid attention to this battered warrior who had inexplicably come to me.

Now I look and even listen to the rock I carelessly wrap my rope around to secure my raft to the shore of the Deschutes River, use to hold down tent corners camping in the desert, use to create a fire pit, dislodge on my annual ascent up South Sister, skip across high mountain or landlocked desert lakes, rub on my heel to smooth calluses. I pay attention to the rocks that line my Central Oregon chimney or create the pockmarked wall between my neighbor and me or the ones I cast aside in irritation when gardening. Because I now know one might be offering a directional signal—or extending a hand in sympathy or support. There's more to this rockhounding than meets the eye.

# The Old Hackleman Place: An Obituary

EACH SUMMER I TAKE A SENTIMENTAL JOURNEY—head out into the high desert, turn north out of Brothers, and drive deep into Oregon's "outback," deep into the brittle-boned, bake-oven, parched-earth desert, finally reaching a ridge that looks down on an emerald valley, strikingly green running up against the sere yellow hillsides of cheat- and bunchgrass. I sit down on a rock, a vestige of some millennial volcano or fossilized ocean sand (out here it could be either), my lofty perch putting me eye-to-eye with the red-tailed hawks cruising the updraft, lazily looking for the sage rats that flee a swather in the meadow far below as it cuts the ripe hay, leaving it in neat, parallel windrows. This is my annual pause and reflect, a chance to contemplate my life now and to muse on my past experiences in the rough embrace of that beloved, dusty ranch where I once lived. While I do, I leaf through my new copy of the *Oregon Road and Recreation Atlas* to look for familiar landmarks, to confirm that the map agrees I am where I think I am. I'm stunned to discover it doesn't, that the designation of "Hackleman Ranch" has been removed. The longtime map locator for where I lived as a newlywed, carried three children, raised a family, and watched a husband become invisible to himself was gone.

"Where did you say your ranch was again?" a local might ask in conversation. If I give geographic indicators—the South Fork of the Crooked River, north of Buck Creek, between Little and Willow buttes—he looks slightly dissatisfied. I can see his mind trying to home in on the exact location, maybe coming up with an image of a dried-up reservoir on Twelve Mile Flat where he'd camped during the last antelope season. "No, not there exactly," I say. Or maybe the unnatural gash Camp Creek carves through the meadow of crested wheat near Logan Butte. "Close," I say, "but not quite. A few miles more to the west." Visibly disappointed he can't see in his mind's eye exactly where I am talking about, he shrugs off the effort with, "I think I got a rough idea of where you mean."

But if I say "the old Hackleman place," his face lights up with recognition. He pictures the plunge and curve of the road off the rim, the way the two-story house sits at the head of the valley, its windows squinting into the sun. Neither of us speaks for a bit. I happily indulge myself with memories of the joyful pell-mell of my mornings there, ranch hands at the breakfast table, a baby on my hip, a toddler and ranch dogs underfoot, my stomach swelling with new life, the sizzle of bacon and eggs. He nods slowly, given an excuse to recall what he had heard about the original ranch owners—tiny, tidy Margaret managing the place after her husband, Abe Hackleman, died young. Stories of her brother Claude trapped for a day under a capsized tractor, miraculously surviving but losing a leg. His place used to be shown as the "Coffelt Ranch" on the map, just down the valley from the Hackleman, moored safely inside an embrace of steep rimrocks. Now, I notice, that place name has also been dropped from my new road atlas.

Inheriting the original owner's name along with a ranch was like being knighted, honored, passed the baton, entrusted with something precious. If their experience had ended badly you felt it your obligation to right it. If their experience had gone well, you felt an obligation to continue that legacy. If the grass glistened green and the ditches were weed free and the barn upright when you got there, you wanted to leave it as you found it. Or better, if you could. And it guaranteed that you would inherit lots of anecdotal history about the place where you now lived. Just make mention of "the old Hackleman place" and you would hear, whether you wanted to or not, had time for it or not, about the sisters-in-law, Margaret and Dorothy, fighting at Margaret's mailbox with their umbrellas over Margaret's accusation that Dorothy cut the fence between their places to let her wild-eyed, slack-jawed cattle graze Margaret's lush grass. Dorothy Hackleman. She never married. "Nobody crazy enough to marry her," was the opinion expressed by those who knew of her antics. It was said she herded cattle in her car, kept all her money in cash under the seat, died in the Prineville hotel fire.

"The old Hackleman Place," he'll repeat, coming out of his reverie, interrupting mine. "So you must be that gal from back east. Now I remember. You and your husband are the ones bought from Margaret. Met that crazy son-of-a-bitch husband of yours. Liked him. Damn straight. Helluva cowboy. He got kind of carried away with the drugs and booze. Sure sorry about that." By the standards of desert etiquette he wasn't being rude or intrusive, instead just doing his job of updating the lore associated with a specific

I take a break during a cattle drive

location. He was acknowledging a more recent chapter that now was part and parcel of "the old Hackleman place," was now embodied in that geographic designation and, as much as any natural occurrence, shaped the sharp cleft of the valley, wrote the melody the cottonwoods sang in the wind.

Over time, family ranch names became synonymous with a certain landscape, with a certain lay of the land, attaching themselves to the red shale and bunchgrass and wild rye of the place. "Dorothy's" came to mean apple trees, aspen groves, the slim ankles of the Maury Mountains revealed behind her place, the bold Ponderosa spires visible on the higher elevations. Dorothy's was always referred to as Dorothy's, Margaret's as "the old Hackleman Place." Though only a few miles removed from Dorothy's, how different the landscape at the Hackleman: the over-generous vistas (I could spot guests coming off the ridge and have the bed sheets changed before they pulled up at the door), the lanky, bare-banked South Fork of the Crooked River. No frilly willow collar for this tributary—rather a ragged lightning strike of blue water that reeled back and forth across the breadth of the valley. Cowboys from this part of the desert didn't much like Dorothy's end of things, all those narrow, forested draws, snarls of pine, mountain mahogany, and underbrush. They favored the long view, where a person could see for miles, ride at a lope all the daylight hours.

Oceanographer Jean Jacques Cousteau theorized that the horizon we look at affects how we think. His a saltwater ocean, this an ocean of sagebrush. The long view. Steady, calm. I have come to believe we are led to the landscape that can teach us what we need to know. In my case, the learning has taken me awhile, coming from a tight, stone-walled, densely wooded New England. I have been slow to learn from this patient, stare-down place where land meets sky halfway. But I am getting there.

A year or so before her death I learned that Margaret had been placed in a nursing home. The orderly directed me to a frail woman sitting in a wheelchair in the hallway, chin to chest.

"She can't walk?"

"Oh, she can walk alright. Just won't. Ornery, is what she is."

"Are you her caregiver?"

"Day shift I am."

"Do you know her, much about her?"

"Not a thing, except that she's ornery. *Aren't you, Margaret!*" she shouted.

I looked over at Margaret who gave no sign of having heard. I turned back to the nurse, the color rising to my face. "This woman, in case you didn't know, ran a hundred-thousand acre ranch all by herself after her husband died, dressed down lazy hired men, cooked for an army, pulled calves, broke horses, survived blizzards ..."

"After all that, I can see why she's so ornery." And the nurse was on to other things.

I squatted down in front of Margaret. "Margaret? It's Ellie."

"Who are you?" she asked, her left index finger worrying the front of the armrest.

"Ellie. It's Ellie. We bought your place, the old Hackleman place, out in the desert. Remember? I wanted to come and say hello."

She lifted her head slowly, as though it weighed one hundred pounds, as though she had forgotten how to look up and out, all horizons robbed, the long view, the kind she was used to. She studied me through small, cloudy eyes. "The Hackleman."

And for a moment I saw in her gaze a cloudless morning on the desert, snuffy horses bucking and twisting with glee, cows nuzzling their newborn, chickens two-legging it to her chant of "Here chick, chick!" For a moment the smell of sage was bright between us, trumped the stench of urine in this land of TVs, trays, IVs, and shiny linoleum.

"The Hackleman," she repeated.

"The ranch is doing great, Margaret. Thanks to you, all your work."

She nodded. At least I like to think she did, before giving in to abandonment, confusion, and no view or promise of anything. I took her hand. "Are you doing okay?" Her chin was back on her chest. "Margaret. I told the nurse about you. She didn't know..."

"Who are you?" The question was directed at her lap. "Go away!" she shouted at her knees.

On my way out, I stopped at the front desk determined to insist "the old Hackleman place," and all that it implied, on the distracted nurses. I tried to make Margaret's experience—and my own—count for something, as though those nurses were the judge and jury of a life well spent, as though my meaning and Margaret's depended on their being persuaded of it. They weren't interested.

The desert doesn't give a fig about ranch names, place names, me, whether or not I spent time on the South Fork of the Crooked River. The desert is absorbed, but not self-absorbed. It dedicates itself to each moment, without any attachment. But humans are into attachment (another word for suffering, according to the Buddhists), into meaning, our meaning. We attach to how we think our lives are supposed to play out, how we name ourselves. When things take a different turn, we mourn what isn't, sit on ridgetops and muse instead of making the recalibration to what is and the possibility of peace and maybe even joy. The desert instructs that if we spend all our time trying to force our version of things on what is actually taking place, to make our tracks (and namesakes) permanent, we will destroy where we live, literally and metaphorically, as well as our chance at experiencing what is commonly referred to as happiness. The lesson of the desert lies in the commitment of the wobbly-legged, see-me-run calf juxtaposed with the chops-licking, cool hand coyote or the breathless abandon of a fragile desert lily blooming into the crushing hailstorm. If the desert has a memory, it is seasonal, magnetic, moonstruck, and guided. It does certain things at certain times of year. Or tries. Some years the grass does get green again, water does fill summer-dry creeks during the spring snow melt. Obsidian chips are unearthed with the runoff and sparkle like the bright, black eyes of a newborn. There is watchfulness, acceptance, meditation but no evaluation, ranking, judgment. And it is of no matter whether something took place at the corner of Main and Elm streets or at "the old Hackleman place." Just a commitment to go like beautiful, exquisite hell in the time you have. Because in the end, dust to dust. In the end, nothing matters except the one hundred percent of the right now.

With all due respect to the laws of nature, there is, however, one human invention that can help us bridge this black hole in space that we tumble around inside. And, no, it is not one more way of peeing on the rocks and corner posts of our existence, not a way of obtaining more meaning or permanence. But it is pure gold worth mining and offers the added bonus of being endlessly and perpetually self-sustaining and renewing. I refer to the act of naming things and to the history and story that names, in this case family place-names, invoke. Not to attach to, not to guarantee anything, not to self-aggrandize the bearer, but simply to be treasured as the repository of certain "species" of experience.

"The old Hackleman place"—it runs together like a single word and holds within it human and natural history that spans centuries. Now that appellation is off the map. (The Bureau of Land Management office in Prineville explained ranch names were now being removed if the ranches don't border county roads.) As it fades from view, the associated memory links start to atrophy, the stories evaporate, the place reserved in our hearts for the unique emotional experiences triggered by that name seals shut. The complex interconnectedness of human and the natural world that is held and nourished within the moniker disappears. The high desert is full of these invisible grave markers. From Stauffer to Fife, from Sartain to Lister. And what of Native family place-names—what were they, where have they gone? When the language of "the old Hackleman Place" ceases to be actively spoken, and that reference is dug up years from now in some semantic archeological exploration, the earnest archeologist will have no way of retrieving the stories attached to it because all the fragile links to time and people and land and heart will be severed, parked in a wheelchair in a nursing home for forgotten names, and left for dead.

# The Church of the High Desert

JOGGING ALONG A REMOTE DIRT ROAD in northeastern Oregon, I was startled by a crude sign stuck into a steep, shaley bank above the Imnaha River—"Roy's UFO Site" it said. Roy had hand-painted the red letters on the uneven, rough-cut piece of plywood. I understood Roy's need to go to the trouble of making and placing the sign, because when you see a UFO, you don't ever forget the experience. You want to "real time" it, to somehow footnote the event in reality, validate your sanity.

I am generally regarded as a reasonable, between-the-lines person, raised right, socially apt. At least I think I am. Certainly not one of those whackos who believe in UFOs. My only exposure to the phenomenon, aside from what I'd gleaned from the headlines of the *National Enquirer* in line at the grocery store, had been when our county road grader, who maintained the miles and miles of gravel in the far reaches of Crook County, quit. He claimed he had seen one too many "of them UFOs." A jittery kind of guy anyway, he became the brunt of many jokes among the ranchers. "Turn off your flashlight, you'll scare Hank." "Somebody must have spiked his Ovaltine."

But like Roy and Hank, I am a believer. It was around winter solstice, moonless, very dark. I was headed to Bend from the ranch to meet my husband in town for a pre-Christmas party. I was nearing Brothers, approaching the turn onto pavement (Highway 20) when suddenly a brilliant white light enveloped my car. I stopped, dazzled, fascinated. It blanketed my vehicle for what seemed like a long time. In total silence. I was only aware of the light and the silence, nothing else. I couldn't see beyond it, nothing of the sagebrush starkly silhouetted in the glare, nothing of the road ahead of me or behind. The light was all consuming. I wasn't afraid. Instead, awestruck. Then, just as abruptly, the light disappeared. Soundless, instantaneous. It didn't gradually recede, or "drive away." It vanished.

It took me a moment to pull myself together. My hands were shaking, I remember that. I remember starting the car. Come to think of it, I don't remember turning it off. I knew I had seen something amazing and inexplicable, a visitation from the land of Otherness, and was a little rattled. Enough so that shortly after I accessed the highway at Brothers and crested a small hill just past the general store, I jumped out of my skin when I saw a lone juniper tree that a Brothers resident had festooned with Christmas lights. I was certain it was another encounter of the third kind. I related my experience to the well-heeled guests at the party in Bend that evening and to my husband, all of whom looked at me as though maybe I'd been out on the desert too long, needed to get out more often. But for me it was akin to a religious experience. And I have had many in the church of the high desert.

As a young girl I was startled each time my strong, robust father would kneel by my bed to say bedtime prayers, would voluntarily become so diminished, so vulnerable, his forehead resting on his folded hands, waiting patiently for me to conclude my long list of God-blesses including, by name, every horse at the riding stables where I took lessons. On Sundays I attended chapel with my parents at the private boarding school in Massachusetts where they both taught. It was in those days an all-boys school, sixth through twelfth grade. The headmaster, in his white surplice, would give an instructive talk each Sunday—more philosophical discourse than sermon, though the school was founded on Episcopal precepts. Just when I began to appreciate the boon of being a teenage girl on an all-boys campus I was sent away to an all-girls Episcopal school in the White Mountains of New Hampshire. Going away to boarding school was the norm in the New England culture I grew up in, all in the name of good education. At this mountain school a prayer service was held each morning and evening with communion on Wednesday mornings and an elaborate service each Sunday. When I reflect on those churchgoing experiences I realize the primary religious imprint on me was repetition and ritual. And too: the observation of silence, when Otherness was invited into the room.

Reverend William Greenfield was the minister at the St. Andrew's Episcopal Church in Prineville when I first moved to our ranch in the high desert. I'd make the long trip into town on some Sundays to savor the familiar interplay of rituals and words. I wished for a church closer to my remote location. It was a visit from my parents, and the desire to show them, and persuade myself, that this ranch life, in this place, with this husband, was a civil and civilized lifestyle that led me to undertake reopening the long-boarded-up Paulina Church, forty miles of dirt road and another twenty of pavement from our ranch house.

The structure was (and remains) endearing for its quaintness. It had a grange-hall-with-small-steeple quality about it. No pretension. It had at one time been painted white. It was bold in its assertion of faith, sitting there unembellished on an embankment above the town.

The Paulina church

Simple, Quaker like. It had no need for buttresses and rosette windows. The cathedral was all around it—out the front door the swing of lush meadows to the Crooked River backed by rolling hills, and, lauding over it all, the fathomless sky. The church was, as much as anything, an envelope in which to put prayer, an aspect of air framed in wood. What was lacking was the stamp of a priest, a pastor, a minister. So I recruited Reverend William Greenfield to help with the renaissance of this modest place of worship. I put a notice in the window of the Paulina Store, next to announcements about team ropings and potlucks, that the next Sunday the church would be reopened followed by a reception at a nearby ranch.

My husband, parents, and I arrived a couple of hours before the service was to begin. They stayed on the front porch of the Paulina General Store and kept our two-year-old entertained while I headed for the church armed with broom and dust cloth. With the key provided me by the general store owner I opened the long-neglected building to confront inches of dust, pack rat debris, and decades-worth of cobwebs hanging like tattered lace doilies. When Reverend Greenfield pulled up in front of the church after his drive from Prineville, it must have looked as though the Holy Ghost was exiting the building, so much dust was billowing out in front of my broom. Mr. Greenfield, a gruff man of over six feet and ample girth, strode inside, surveyed the scene and, to his credit, unfazed, promptly fashioned a communion rail with chairs turned backwards to the congregation. I made one final sweep and wiped off the straight-backed benches. The Reverend gave me copies of the *Book of Common*

*Prayer* to distribute. He then proceeded to dress to the religious nines for the occasion, donning first the white surplice, then chasuble, then the tippet decorated with shields and pins, including from his years in the Canadian Royal Air Force. People began to arrive, pulling up in their pickups, the beds filled with bales of hay, cow dogs perched on top. From the looks on their faces when they first caught sight of Reverend Greenfield looming in the doorway of the church, gussied up the way he was, he may as well have been a UFO.

I had made one crucial error. Before embarking on this mission I failed to take any inventory of the religious preferences of the community. I quickly learned, given the reaction to real wine offered at communion and black coffee at the reception, it was primarily conservative Baptist. But ultimately it was the silent prayer that drew us all together. And in the end, Reverend Greenfield seemed a worthy, though to some unlikely, postmaster of the petitions each in the congregation directed heavenward.

Despite that inauspicious start, the church has remained open over thirty years now, with pastors of various denominations making the trek, taking turns leading the service each Sunday, guiding the quest for making sense out of the senseless, teasing out the meaning of the Mystery, the Other out of the silence.

I never was one for the realistic appraisal of things. What it would take to clean out the Paulina Church, for one. My fantasies about my husband, our marriage, and ranch life together, for another. I never anticipated, was not prepared for the fact that things could turn out badly, that the possibility even existed. And I came late to realizing that investing my energy in the fact they *had* in some ways turned out badly was not the best use of my energetic dollar, and, most importantly, was not my only option.

When I came to understand this it was close to a religious conversion. It happened in one of the many anecdotal, accidental places of worship scattered all over the high desert, with rye grass for walls, sky for clerestory, lava rocks for altar. It happened after my fantasies about what my life would be like had been systematically demolished by my experience.

I am persuaded notions about how one's life will turn out, or should have, are false gods. It's easy to "worship" them and by that I mean organize our lives around them, make assumptions about them, missing what is happening peripherally in our lives that may offer clues and road signs to the direction we should be going, to the message we should be gleaning from our life-walk. Anything, I have concluded, that causes regret or self-pity is a sure sign one is holding too tight to a fantasy about one thing or another.

For me the realization took place seated on a rocky promontory with thousands of gnarled lava fingers, like church spires, sticking up through a canopy of mountain mahogany and juniper. I had hiked to this spot in the Hart Mountain Antelope Refuge in a state of deep melancholy, certain that life was asking me to be numb and passive, that there wasn't a place for the all of me to show up. That my life was hard, nothing more. If the rocks and dried earth around my feet were any indication, the landscape seemed to agree with me, except for one thing: a flower, blooming blue flax, pushing up through the rubble. No, it said in its small, bright voice. No. This is exactly the soil you require to grow, to blossom. Pay attention. Trust. Then the moment wrapped me in a soft, comforting wind shawl and laid its sun-warmed hands on my head.

The pristine silence of the desert holds what I need to return to myself. Native Americans understand that in nature, they walk within the cathedral of Great Spirit, of God. They understand the teachings of the earth, its language of silence, of Otherness. Silence is not an awkwardness, something to be avoided or filled, but rather sought out for the instruction it contains. A Lakota Sioux medicine man holds sweat lodge ceremonies near Bend, encourages non-Indians to participate. So I did. Though many Natives would not agree, he wants to share the traditions of his people to encourage others to follow the Red Path or, at least, gain a better understanding of the Native American view of things.

The sweat lodge was made of layers of tarps secured to a ribcage of bent willows. The path to the entrance was marked by two parallel rows of small, round gray stones. Prior to going in, the handful of us participating in the ceremony sat cross-legged on the ground and in silence tied tobacco pouches: black representing the west, for strength and guidance; red the north, for healing; yellow the east, for introspection; white the south for love, compassion. We tied blue for Father Sky and all winged creatures, green for Mother Earth and purple for the all-encompassing infinite Spirit. I carefully placed a pinch of tobacco in each small square of colored cloth, then tied them to a string, a necklace of multi-colored amulets. A fire had been built the night before outside the lodge and large lava rocks heated in it. The heat of the stones, I was told, carried love into the sweat lodge. They were red-hot now, hot enough to be glass, to form clear black obsidian.

Before closing the entrance with the tarp and enveloping us in total darkness, the leader explained what each round signified. In the first round seven stones are placed in the fire and doused with water and "calling songs" are chanted to the spirits and ancestors. The second round, the prayer round, more hot stones are added and each person offers his or her personal supplications concluding with: "homitakuye oyasin" or "all my relations." The third round, the hottest, the hardest, is the suffering round, signifying the willingness of those participating in the sweat to suffer, so others will not have to. The Native belief that dedicated suffering is sublime and painless is also exemplified in the Sundance ceremony, in which men dance for a week, without food, attached to a central pole by a strip of cherry wood whittled sharp and inserted under the muscles in their chests. In the fourth round of the sweat, the door is briefly opened to let in some cool air, the pipe is passed, and then the flaps are closed again for the final round—filled with songs and chants to send the spirits home again, to thank and release them.

The medicine man presiding over the ritual was huge. His graying black braid lay across his shoulder like a piece of discarded rope. His naked belly rested on his thighs. His chest bore numerous small scars striated in quick, short strokes, evidence of the many Sun Dance ceremonies he had done. He talked about the sweat lodge being the equivalent of a church, and that in the Native tradition the spiritual is accessed through the body. The darkness in the lodge, he explained, allowed us to become one with the darkness, with each other, with everything.

Once the entrance was sealed not a trace of light entered. Two large ladles of water were poured over the first seven rocks and the steam began to build. With the intense, humid heat, and the total darkness I quickly ceased to be aware of anyone, anything. I shed my clothes and let the sweat pour off my arms, my nipples, my forehead. No one could see me and I could see no one, could not make out one detail of my hand when I held it in front of my face. I lost myself to the space, the darkness. Some joined in the prayer rounds, others collapsed onto the damp ground to escape the heat that rose and nested inside the cervix of the lodge.

After the final round, I pulled my clothes around me and crawled out into the night. I encountered hardly a night, hardly a darkness, compared to where I had been. Where was that? The darkness, like silence, was not an enclosure, but a vast and limitless space. It is, perhaps, the space we are asked to travel each day—in trust, in faith, in love, even when you can't see, can't hear.

Most aboriginal cultures understand that listening and taking cues from the earth's heartbeat reveal other energies, instructions. They seem to know better than most that one must get silent in order to hear, that entering the void is the only way to be reminded of our relative stature. Listening to the play of the breeze in a cluster of aspen or the rush of water over smooth rocks is primordial, womblike, returns us to the subconscious aquifer of our being, allows us to recall innocence and absolute trust, allows us to re-emerge renewed. We white folk seem to operate on few of the available spiritual cylinders, constrict our hearts in the name of God, rather than open them.

On a bike trip through the Pine Creek conservation area, between Antelope and Condon we passed towering cliffs of solidified volcanic mayhem and fossilized tributes to fantastical climates, flora and fauna of old. A fellow cyclist stepped over to a roadside sign and called out what it said.

"Listen to this!" she announced enthusiastically. "These palisades are forty million years old. How amazing."

In awe we flopped our helmeted heads back and stared up at the steeples of lava that seemed to be toppling over in front of the clouds scudding behind them. As we walked back to the road to resume our ride a woman from behind the steering wheel of a parked car yelled out: "They are not forty million years old. They can't be. God made them."

Why was I in Imnaha River country, running along that dirt road where I happened upon Roy's sign? I was on an extended writing retreat complete with a lakeside cabin. While on this sojourn I met a Buddhist monk of the Soto Zen tradition. Reverend Tuttle had lived in a monastery in California for many years before answering a call to somewhere in northeastern Oregon. That somewhere turned out to be Wallowa County. The first year, she converted the living room of a rented ranch house into a temple. People, myself included, began attending her weekly meditations. By the second year, she had received a gift of acreage and a house where the Wallowa Buddhist Temple is now located. When I sit in meditation with her I feel certain Reverend Tuttle can hear the din of my mind's chatter, the thoughts careening and ricocheting around in my head like sniper fire. But the more I sit, on my own or when I have the opportunity to be with Reverend Tuttle, the more I see the chatter in my mind as aspects of the grasp-and-cling dance, the vestments of fantasy. In the meditative silence she creates, Reverend Tuttle joins with Native elders in nature, with priests in cathedrals and Reverend Greenfields in small, rural churches engaged in silent prayer, all making room for Other, for Buddha, for Great Spirit, for God to enter. Reverend Tuttle gave me this invocation:

*The gift of the light of the Lord is everywhere.*
*The palace of the Buddha nature is within ourselves.*
*The deep, true heart wants to go quickly*
*so their happy reunion will occur soon.*

Is it blasphemy to give prayer and airtime to these seemingly contradictory religious and spiritual currents? I now believe it doesn't matter so much how each of us get there (or should I say There?), so long as we do. So long as we seek to discern the Other, the holy in all things. I recently caught the reflection of a light bulb in a window. The reflection was diffused—not finely etched, not really the thing itself but confirmation of the existence of the real thing somewhere. This, to me, is faith. See the reflection of the holy, the Godly contained in all living things and thus know for sure the real thing is somewhere out there.

I have taken a circuitous route to this point, my religious actualization hampered by my humanness, my propensity to doubt, over-analyze. The perfect obstruction to faith and surrender is the desire to know for sure, to really know. I can say finally I believe in God. I understand the difference between pain (inevitable) and suffering (optional). Understand what was unleashed by choosing choice (and therefore consequence) as everyman and everywoman exited the Garden of Eden. Understand what the single most important task is in life—to transform suffering. Make the world more than we are, more than itself. Forgiveness for the unforgivable. The cohabitation of impossible beauty and impossible hardship. The road to embracing the mystery is paved with silence. My sense of the godhead has become more and more discernible through the dust of time, of life, billowing out of that Paulina church.

I still go to the Episcopal church some Sundays. And too, when I drive the empty high desert roads at night I am always on the lookout for UFOs if for no other reason than they confirm we aren't the only game in town, be they alien or angel. I welcome being stopped in my tracks by Otherness. I know Roy, and I think even Hank, would agree.

# That's Deep

PEOPLE WHO HAVE ALWAYS LIVED with an ear close to the land, an eye trained on distant horizons, hear and see things differently. Take Jack. He died a few years ago at the age of ninety-one, in July, just before it was time to gather his cattle off summer pasture. He had ranched the same ranch outside of Mitchell all his life.

Although Mitchell's Pink Spur Bar has been closed for years, until recently the sign swung catawampus at the end of a single rusty strand of chain, gaudy and rakish. The general store and post office, the tire shop, and the nine-room Oregon Hotel are still open for business, sluggish as it may be. The owner of the Little Pine Truck Stop keeps a live brown bear in a cage next to the gas pumps. He's had it since it was a cub. He only recently decided it wasn't safe to go inside the cage to feed the enormous, hapless critter. The buildings are clustered on a loop road that half-moons off Highway 26. The town is like someone in intense meditation. Breathing and the passage of time have nearly stopped. The main but little-traveled road goes on to Fossil, Izee, Suplee, John Day, remote locations in Oregon's outback, Oregon's high desert.

Mitchell's claim to fame is that it's an access point for the Painted Hills. They're like a color-coded ant farm—chapters in geology and paleontology vividly revealed in the side-cut of the hills. The green layer holds fossilized record of ancient waterfowl and shells that left their concentric or lacey ribbed print in the rock. Yellow reveals the giant tusk of the mastodon or jaw of the saber-toothed cat. The blue sediment retells two million years of the fossil history of animals who, as Ellen Bishop states in her book *In Search of Ancient Oregon*, "never saw one another and are a thousand generations or more apart." Ten thousand years ago native populations first roamed the land, fashioned sandals out of sage bark, and fished for the spawning salmon out of Cherry Creek. The damp caves secluded in the creases of the hillsides sheltered them and provided rough canvas for their petroglyphs. The Indians left behind telltale obsidian arrowheads that caught the glint of the afternoon sun and the eye of the white folks who homesteaded the area.

The white settlers found that the hardy bunchgrasses around Mitchell were loaded with protein for their cattle. Creeks there ran year around. The John Day River coursed between the rainbow hills. It was easy gathering off the high country and down the draws that cinched in the valley like a belt. Microclimates got boxed into the canyons. Things grew there that others in the high desert only dreamed of— peaches, plums. Even corn and tomatoes had a fair chance.

Jack's ranch had achieved such a perfect balance: an abundance of water, wildlife, mountain summer pasture, and meadows overwhelmed with alfalfa or dry land rye. Cows certainly loved it. Always weaned big calves. Mother cows bred back consistently. "I warn my girls," Jack would say. "Come up empty and you'll be shipped. Guess none of them want to leave."

Trailing cows all those years in and around Mitchell country, Jack had developed some "settin' in the saddle" theories. Tilting his porch chair, rolling a toothpick back and forth across his mouth, he'd venture one or two. Like the fact that a cow and her calf will always return to where they last sucked. So even if they get split up, hauled off miles in separate directions, they will find their way back to that very spot. He knew of cows that forded rivers, broke through fences to return to where they last gave milk, when careless cowboys had accidentally separated pairs. He'd go on to speculate how humans did the same. Figured most of the time folks spent on some psychiatrist's couch was trying to figure out just where that spot was they were last truly nourished. He believed knowing when you've been nurtured and by whom was critical—and that it had to take place in regular increments, at certain formative points in your life, or "a calf turns lepy, a person lonely." Or how any species that gets too fancy for its own good is headed for extinction. "Over-armored or over-ornamented. It's the start of *sayonara*. Worried about folks these days— mobile what's-its, SUVs. They seem to think it's all necessary, get 'em somewhere they aren't. They forget. Grass is always greener where it's watered."

But there was one theory of Jack's I found the most compelling and, like the others, he had come up with it up trailing a bunch of black baldy yearlings off the high country. As Jack put it: "When you're young, very young, time goes by *real* slow but the metabolism is hell bent. As you get older, time speeds up and the metabolism slows down considerable. At death's door," and here Jack got pretty excited, "the metabolism stops altogether, and yet time goes by so fast that all your life's experiences flash before you in one single, fleeting moment." He removed his sweat-stained cap, slicked back his gray hair with the hand missing a forefinger thanks to a run-in with the tractor, and replaced the cap on his head. "What," he asked me, "do you make of that?"

I've been turning that one over till the edges are worn smooth. According to Jack's theory it would seem at some point the arcing ellipses of time and metabolism must intersect and when they do, should be in exquisite balance and harmony. Do you suppose this intersection is a single moment in our life? If so, it must be one of near perfection. How can we know when it is? How can we know when we're in it? Or is it a particular quality within each moment? If I get really good, can I stay at that intersection and experience everything that way? Could I experience my whole life like the moment when the fly line dances out over the river, before it hits the water? Before a baby takes in its first breath on the way to a life-affirming cry? The time between the coyote's laugh leaving its lips and when I hear it on the other side of the valley? Just before I wake from a dream? Is it the moment just before we express our love—the expression of it waiting just backstage anticipating its entry? Can we only recognize these moments in hindsight? Like salt thrown over the shoulder for good luck? Or can we live in the present and immediate knowledge of these moments eternally, by practicing, by nurturing an awareness that they are always happening around us, until it is the all and only of life?

These are some of the questions I was fixing to ask Jack while gathering cattle off his summer pasture ... the July he died.

# PauMau

NEVER TAKE LONGER TO GET SOMEWHERE than you'll stay once you do. That was the maxim and one of the reasons why the monthly PauMau Women's Club meetings lasted at least two hours. Nothing to drive twenty to forty miles of dirt road each way. Depending on the season, could be gumbo, "slicker than snot," or frozen, rutted tire tracks that violently bucked vehicles side to side. Come summer, desert dust fine as flour. Slam the car door shut and the brown powder would slide off the car like a women's silk nightgown. Each woman carried seasonal strategies in her truck bed or car trunk: chains, shovel, spare tire and jack, a winch, an old plastic gallon jug filled with water. And always a bar of soap or pack of gum stashed in the glove box, quick fixes for punctures in the gas tank or radiator. The ladies would get airborne over the metal cattle guards, dangly earrings flying. In a hurry to get there, to the meetings. Especially this one. It was the Christmas potluck and gift exchange.

PauMau. That's for Paulina and Maury Mountains. The official clubhouse was in Paulina. Well not exactly "in" Paulina, not included in the downtown "business loop" as the sign read, a designation suggesting something much grander than the crescent-shaped quarter-mile detour off the numberless road cupping the community church, general store, dance hall, a few houses, and the elementary school. Instead, the clubhouse perched on the lip of the thin rural thoroughfare that traveled the berm above the settlement and trailed off aimlessly into the desert.

They made the drive from isolated places, for some from very lonely places, but all of them rugged and beautiful places decorated with draws and swales pocked with bunchgrass; acres of quarreling sage and rabbitbrush; haphazard juniper stands or high-stepping rows of poplar; hay meadows crisscrossed by creeks with necklaces of willow stringing alongside; steep ridges traced by coyotes on a lazy prowl; eagles and redtails making light of updrafts; or an abandoned barn moping into the hillside, rotted gray beams sticking unnaturally and violently straight into the sky. Shaley hillsides covered with cheatgrass showed off bright green in early spring and then settled into a summer-long whisper of yellow ground cloth. Late fall—treeless, windy flats easily twelve miles end-to-end rendered speechless by a hard frost and a skiff of snow with a startle of antelope streaking zebra brown, black, white across. The high desert country is flat beautiful. That's all there is to it.

Every month. The women. The women meet, eager for the chatter, banter, chitchat. Their talk—rich, strong, to-the-point, full of freewheeling grammatical shortcuts. They're the backboard, the ballast, the balance for their ranch's operation and know it, though wouldn't say so. Day in and day out, each toils as a one-woman service organization, working alongside and for men: husbands, fathers, fathers-in-law, hired men. Whole worlds, lifetimes, come and go between PauMau get-togethers. Especially and maybe only at club meetings can they bask in the solace of ranch women together, relax into the embrace of other women who know firsthand about their style of living.

On their way, the women drive by what to anyone who didn't know the country, didn't live there, would seem unremarkable. But that corner was right where Irene hit the deer driving home alone from town with her firstborn. Jumped out, grabbed the rifle mounted behind the seat, and shot the deer in the head to put it out of its misery. "Almighty keepin' the score even, I guess," she speculated out loud at the next club meeting. And there—Ellie took a snowy curve one night and came straight into a cavvy of horses on the road. Their eyeballs rolled white with fear as they pitched up and over the hood of her car. They survived it. So did she. That butte with the red rock apron? That's where, setting a line of traps, Van found saber-toothed tiger bones. Helen made him promise not to tell the university folks for fear of being overrun. And the BLM allotment, the one they seeded with crested wheat—that's where old Ronnie turns out any of his rodeo stock that won't buck. In their green government trucks, binoculars around their necks, BLM-ers spot the rank, sway-backed, parrot-nosed crow-hoppers, get all excited, enter them in the

PauMau Club founders

wild horse count, round them up for adoption come spring. Can just spot the roof of Mary's place. Her husband had been dead probably a year when the waterspout flash-flooded the side of the hill right through her living room. Mary, seventy-six, frail as a spinet, swam through mud and tree roots to the stairs, over-handed her way up the fluted wooden rail to avoid being swept away by the tsunami of debris that ravaged her home. She'll be at the meeting. Fence ahead marks the south boundary of a place just bought up by some absentee owner. So much of that now. Eroding the community faster than the spring runoff collapses the banks of the Crooked River. It's a shame. Can't hardly make a living ranching anymore. The men joke they're in it for the psychic income. Most will hold on as long as they can, but those big city hobby farmers throw money around like never. That's Carolyn's there. She operates a beauty parlor in her spare room. Also drives bus for the elementary school. More and more, the women needing to find paid work. Carolyn's buying all kinds of nice things. "No one give it to me," she says proudly, showing off her new crockpot. Carolyn has an old pet sow that wanders into the salon now and then for a scratch behind her bristly ear. Rolls her huge self over, shamelessly exposing rows of leathery tits, right at the feet of the women with their hair in rollers, seated under large, noisy dryer hoods shouting at each other. The road south leads to the ranch of the no-account who imported brucellosis into the upper country. Trading low-grade cattle is what he was doing. State had him shoot all his calves, ship the females for slaughter. Way he neglected his fences, miracle it didn't spread. His wife attends club. She's got a counterfeit for a husband, that's all there is to it. At PauMau some things are talked about, some aren't.

The Christmas gathering, unlike the other meetings that just serve coffee and dessert, is a meal. The hostesses make ham and turkey, the rest bring salad and dessert and a gift to put under the artificial tree decorated with strung cranberries and cutout snowflakes. Beans, Jell-O salad, scalloped potatoes, apple crisp. The old two-gallon coffee pot rattles and quakes in the kitchen as it brews fresh. Everyone is dressed up. Elaborate rhinestone-tipped glasses, feather earrings, velour sweaters. Some wear heels that neatly pierce the ground as they walk from their rig to the one-room clubhouse or to the outhouse out behind. PauMau women could likely walk dainty in high heels across any kind of terrain. Same as they can open and close the door with a simultaneous pull and swing, with the matter-of-fact agility of someone who has done lots of hard physical work, known hope, and weathered heartbreak, wielded a branding iron or vaccine gun, waved their husband through countless gates, cradled a colicky child, ridden the buck out of a mare, forgiven a drunk spouse, straddled an orphaned calf, its head propped between her knees, and insisted warm milk from a nippled bottle, or endured the unstoppable affection of bummer lambs who have imprinted her as their mother, now always underfoot, bleating, trotting after her as she feeds pigs and chickens.

The secretary and treasurer's reports were fair conversational game. So was planning for special events: the annual Paulina Rodeo, for example, held Labor Day weekend each year. Anyone can enter. It's one of the few left that's open to amateurs who want to try their luck team-roping or lasting eight seconds astride an ornery ranch bull or rank, proud-cut gelding. At PauMau a person could talk about getting new indoor-outdoor carpet or La-Z-Boy, so long as the home tuning wasn't too fine, too fancy considering the bleak, single-wide conditions some of the hired women lived in, or about a trip planned to Reno so long as it wasn't too high fallutin' out of respect to those who had never left the county. Could talk weather, beauty tips, and, of course, stories of labor and delivery. Listening to them, it's a miracle anyone dared to have a child. Could talk ranch gossip so long as it was a county or so removed ("Hear Bernard's hired man up and died there towards John Day. Archie found him in the bunkhouse dead as a nit"). Could talk babies. Could comment ("Jim's singing soprano now, will be standing tall in the saddle for a few days") or complain in a distant, generic way about husbands. On this topic especially, those listening never volunteered an opinion. No one agreed or disagreed, just a nod of acknowledgement. After years of meeting like this, the women knew what not to talk about—such as cattle that had come up missing, downed fence, equipment and even hearts borrowed, returned broken or sometimes lost forever.

When it was time for the gift exchange, ornately wrapped presents were passed around. Neither giver nor intended receiver was identified. Worked best that way. Once everyone had a package, squeezing it, shaking it next to her ear, speculating as to the contents, the hostess ordered they be passed, passed again, reversed by one, and twice more. If anyone ended up with her own, she exchanged with her neighbor. From inside the excited frenzy of paper and tissue and ribbons emerged crocheted pot holders, homemade chutney, a knit scarf or quilted pillow slip, a macramé plant hanger or a set of recipes in a handmade booklet bound with thick yarn. Everyone expressed pleasure in what she got. Not everyone always meant it. The gifts were tucked neatly under the gray folding metal chairs and the table cleared for the craft project.

This year Styrofoam forms in the shape of a Christmas tree were passed around. In the middle of the table: cans of gold spray paint and a pile of dried Russian thistle, the soft tufted blossom nestled inside the boney fortress of razor-sharp, curling spikes. Each woman cut the stalks, careful to avoid the long barbs, and stuck the dried heads into the Styrofoam until the form was completely covered. Then the thistles were spray-coated in solid gold—all the irregularities, the hooks and arrows, the nears and misses, transformed into something of beauty, glossed over, salved with shiny, golden lacquer. When everyone was done, everything cleaned up, the meeting was adjourned. Each woman left with her gift, and a brightly burnished keepsake of gentled thorns to place on her kitchen table, to tide her over until next month when she'd hightail the dirt miles to PauMau.

# Last Log

ON SEPTEMBER 9, 1993, A CROWN PACIFIC "Memo To Employees" announced that the last large log would be processed through the mill that day at noon, signaling the final closure of that portion of mill operations. The informal plan was to allow each station operator the opportunity to perform his task one last time—loader, trimmer, debarker, scaler, sawyer, edger, filer, green chain, stacker, and planer. It is not clear whether the mill management realized how important this impromptu ceremony would prove to be. Western corporate culture isn't known for recognizing the need for rituals—to celebrate beginnings, to give thanks, to grieve endings. Likewise, millworkers and loggers aren't credited for placing much stock in such events. And anyway, who would have thought this day would ever come?

After all, since 1915, lumber mills had defined Bend's skyline: towering smoke stacks, massive wooden basilicas, wigwam burners, and railroad transoms. The timber industry provided the economic blood that gave life to the young town, attracting scores of workers from the Midwest—family man and outdoorsman, adventurer and artisan—to fell trees or process logs. Work in the woods and in the mills was a way of life that boasted its own language, dress, and customs and had put bread on the table of generations of Central Oregonians.

In 1984 the City of Bend requested that the mill stop sounding the shift whistle, due to the numbers of complaints from white collar newcomers to the growing community. When the whistle went mute, little did anyone realize what that silence foretold. This was well before the spotted owl was a subject of household debate; before Earth First radicals sank shards of metal into tree trunks to intentionally cause injury, or even death, to the logger whose saw struck the rogue metal; before zealots were camped in treetops, a human sacrifice to the preservation of a tree.

But sure enough, nine years later in August of 1993, Crown Pacific was forced to announce the closure of the large log portion of the Bend mill. It seemed every day that year a mill closed somewhere in Oregon, economically and emotionally crippling entire communities overnight. In Bend, local workers and loggers alike wanted to believe that at least the small mill portion of the Bend operation would continue to run. But anyone who took the time could see that the supply of raw material, regardless of the stump diameter, was dwindling due to stricter and stricter enforcement of cutting regulations, and that environmental victories had resulted in the prohibition of logging across enormous tracts of federal forest throughout the region. The small mill would close four months later.

The day the last large log was milled was almost disrespectful in its sunny, crisp, carefree giddiness, as days in that high desert community are at that time of year. The gigantic, yellow front-end loader, gripping the enormous girth of the Ponderosa in its talons, waddled on its massive cat tracks toward the belt that would receive the log and start it on its journey through the mill. Men in work boots, T-shirts, and overalls lined the ramp that skirted the belt, watching in respectful silence. The log crashed mightily down off the loader into the cradle of the conveyor. The gears were thrust into forward, the wheels and cogs reluctantly starting to turn, screeching and wailing in protest as if they knew.

The log was forced through the trimmer and debarker, emerging white and pure, its round promise coming to a stop at the entrance to the dark interior of the mill. The conveyor belt was abruptly shut down, whining to a halt. Then, in startling silence, uninterrupted, not even by a cough or shuffle of feet, eighty-eight-year-old former forester Hans Milius stepped up to scale the log. In his hand he held a long, wooden measuring device with a sharp hook on one end, designed to grab the outside perimeter of the log. As the acknowledged elder and the barker of the log's last rites, he solemnly and deliberately called out the log's dimensions. He then passed the measuring stick, like a runner in a slow motion relay, to another and then another, each younger than the previous, so that anyone who had ever done this job could have his final turn, confirming, as Hans had, that this was a big, beautiful, and generous pine, whose bounty would raise many a roof in and around the whole of the Northwest.

Just as suddenly the belt was started up again, and this time the head sawyers took turns slicing the log into boards. The first one stepped into the glassine-covered booth that looked like the control cab of a Ferris wheel. He took pains to carefully hone the outside of the boards to straight dimensions, swiveling on the chair, deftly wielding the gears, as the log rocked dumbly back and forth, more finely tuned with each pass. And then, as though choreographed in advance, the next sawyer, and then another, wordlessly stepped in behind, taking a last turn at his task that had for years meant clothes for the kids, a new ski boat, a pickup truck, the dishes the wife wanted, the La-Z-Boy, a VCR, tuition for the first in the family to attend college, or money for Saturday nights at the show.

Working in a small garret above were the band saw filers. The thirty-foot-long steel saw below them spun faster than the speed of sight, its offset metallic teeth gnawing furiously and surgically through the center of the log. Replacement blades lay in waiting, loose and languid on the floor of the dimly lit workspace. The specialized skill of the band saw sharpener determined the kerf, or width, of the saw cut. The wider, the more waste. Every filer prided himself on his own technique for producing no kerf. Like everyone who worked the mills, he knew there was no place for waste in this profession. Tuned, the freshly sharpened saw was fed to the sawyer through a hole in the floor of the attic hideaway, then lifted onto the feeder belt and secured into position. At the flick of the switch the saw leapt back to lethal life, cutting the log cleanly in half again.

At each station the log's significance increased in proportion to its diminishing size. Each time the gears were stopped, the real and symbolic significance of the mighty partnership of man and machine was framed by the silence, as immense as the interior of the mill itself. The working men who crammed the scaffold that crisscrossed the loft of the building wept silently. Stilled, these huge wheels and pulleys were robbed of their empowering companion—like the skeleton of a mastodon robbed of its flesh and breath. The suggestion of power, but only the suggestion, remained. Both the machines and the men were diminished, were less for it. Less machine. Less man.

The log now lay cut into smooth, white, stacked planks, ready for the dry kiln. The machines and cranes and saws and belts in the large log mill on the banks of the Deschutes River were silenced forever. But the men assembled there, with no prompting, engaged in a last act of defiance against the course of history. As one, they moved toward the pulley that triggered the shift whistle. They pulled hard on the rope, and the whistle sounded long and sang loud of the machines and the men who operated them, offered shrill thanks to the evergreen forests that surrounded them. When finally it stopped sounding, the men let out a gruff, uneven cheer, tripped up by their emotions, and wordlessly walked out of the building, their tin lunch pails and hard hats in hand.

The next Monday, when they showed up for career counseling, the echo of that whistle rang in their ears, like a promise. It continued to sing in their hearts, as they, in the weeks to come, tried to persuade their strong, thick fingers to dance delicately across a keyboard instead of pulling the green chain. This accidental ritual had allowed them to pay homage to the ending of a way of life that was made of them, powered by them—great men of great action, strength, and endurance. They rode the sound of that whistle into the next chapter of their lives not without terrible sadness, but nevertheless comforted in the knowledge that this ending had been duly honored, ritualized, and blessed.

# The Main Thing

Cameron and Don Kerr

I WATCHED THE HIGH DESERT MUSEUM grow from a small office in downtown Bend in the 1970s to the national treasure it is today. Situated on a 135-acre campus, home to outdoor wildlife exhibits and interactive cultural displays, it also boasts 110,000 square feet of interior exhibit space. I had witnessed Don Kerr, against all odds, manage to get the land donated, raise the funds, and build his field of dreams. "Wildly excite, responsibly teach," he was fond of saying. Portland and Central Oregon naysayers ultimately became the strongest supporters of Don Kerr's radical vision for a natural and cultural history museum focusing on the high desert. He pulled it off in grand style, with the groundbreaking in 1979 and the official opening in 1982, bracketing the nation's worst (until now) recession since the Great Depression.

In those days Kerr had the eccentric and distracted demeanor of a man with and on a mission, the charisma of a politician-cum-absentminded professor, which combination charmed many to follow this Pied Piper. He inspired and cajoled people to do things they never dreamed they'd do. Not just write checks or donate land. Ask me how I know this. Ranching in the high desert for more than two decades I found myself, at Don's urging, telling sage rat hunters: "Sure! You can hunt on our property… so long as you deliver the dead ones to me." Handing over their catch, they'd watch in horror as I slipped the bloody, hapless creatures into plastic bags and drop them into the large freezer chest in the boot room of our ranch house. The marksmen hurried away in their trucks, no doubt persuaded the years of living so far out had gotten to me and that sage rat was a new delicacy on my family's menu. The truth was, Don had sent out a request to ranchers to save the frozen ground squirrels for the raptors in captivity at the museum.

As much as the successful launch of the High Desert Museum is testimony to Kerr's single-minded focus, persuasiveness, and energy, its enduring success is testimony to something even greater: the brilliance of Don Kerr's original vision. Twenty-eight years and four directors later, new exhibits continue to best the previous ones. Under the current leadership of museum President Janeanne Upp, 2009 saw the highest-ever number of visitors. The new *Sin in the Sagebrush* exhibit broke all previous records of attendance at an opening. So when the *High Desert Journal* called, I said it would be an honor to write a piece about Don Kerr.

A few days before my scheduled meeting with Don and Cameron, his wife of thirty years, a deer, apparently struck by a car, somehow made its way into my back garden along the Deschutes River in downtown Bend. My house is cheek-by-jowl with other houses, in fact so close that there is only one off-street access to my backyard. That this small doe managed to find this sanctuary amazed me. She nestled in the ground cover under a shrub. I found myself drawn to gaze at her endlessly. I would quietly open the back door and tiptoe across my deck to get as close as I could without frightening her. She would raise her head, ears forward, watching, observing me intently, perfectly and exquisitely silent. "What can I do for you? What do you need? What do you want? Are you alright?" I'd ask. She stared at and through me, her lower jaw moving slowly, chewing on a fragment of thought, of grass. The fourth night, the night before my meeting with Don Kerr, I peeked out the door to say good night. She raised her head and then, before I retreated back into the house, tucked her nose under leg to sleep. The next morning she was gone.

The high desert embraces an approximate area from the Rockies to the Cascades and Sierra, from southern British Columbia to the Great Basin of eastern Oregon and Nevada. "High" because of its altitude, "desert" because of its low rainfall—about twelve inches a year. It's a part of the world where evaporation exceeds rainfall. And in the Great Basin section, the water can't get out, is landlocked. Sitting at a higher latitude and altitude than any other North American desert, it includes everything from pine forests to sand dunes. It accounts for one-fifth of the continental United States and, aside from Alaska, is still the most remote place in America. It is a place where sagebrush lives for one hundred years, hot springs bubbling to the surface of the earth signal its molten center only twenty thousand feet below, and fire circles atop a butte recall a time when Native Americans claimed the desert as their own. The desert and its landscape are an acquired taste. The desert is subtle, secretive in color and movement. It doesn't brandish. To know the high desert requires diving deep into this sagebrush ocean, looking closely, taking time, tasting silence. As American historian Bernard Devoto wrote in *The Year of Decision: 1846*: "Remember that the yield of a hard country is a love deeper than a fat and easy land inspires, that throughout the arid West the Americans have found a secret treasure...a stern and desolate country, a high bare country, a country brimming with beauty not to be found elsewhere."

Don Kerr dove deep and each time he came up for air he had made one more discovery about the magic of the place. As Cameron states: "The museum is Don's invitation to wake up to reality, to go from user to steward or all will disappear." Kerr worked tirelessly to enlist the enthusiasm and support of others. Some donors jokingly recall that the more urgent Don felt about building a new structure or acquiring a unique collection, the more he mumbled. Rather than embarrass themselves by again asking "What did you say?" they nodded in agreement to whatever Don was proposing, which often was a large contribution. That was when he could still talk. He hasn't spoken a word since 1995.

In a tragedy of Shakespearean proportion, Don Kerr contracted encephalitis that year. It is suspected an owl whose talon punctured his handler's glove transmitted the disease. How ironic that one of the very raptors he sought to protect, to educate us all about, would unintentionally be his Judas. So when I went to meet with Don it was his wife Cameron who acted as his mouthpiece. She readily admits she prefers backstage to center stage, never intending to speak on behalf of her husband, but she has not left his side throughout this ordeal, has regally shouldered her responsibilities and accepted the dramatic change in the course of her life. She explains almost matter-of-factly, with complete sincerity and no hint of martyrdom, that when she and Don married they made a pact: "If anything happens to either of us we'll be there."

I pulled up in front of Don and Cameron's house. Three black labs circled their tails in abject delight as they galumphed to greet me. Cameron and Don, in his wheelchair, were at the door. Cameron remarked on how timely I was. She notices that sort of thing. Disciplined. Capable. Organized. Doesn't suffer fools, one would safely assume. She is strong, lean, an accomplished athlete and outdoorswoman. Sixty years have done nothing to compromise her beauty, the striking blue of her eyes. She is a product of both the city and the country—growing up in Vancouver, Washington, her parents later purchasing a ranch in Central Oregon when Cameron was a teenager. She took away a can-do attitude from her ranching experience that serves her now. The long driveway to their house piled up with snow? Nothing for her to get the old pickup started, plow attached, and clear the miles to the county road. Wheel Don out to the wood shop where she is entertaining their six grandsons with her woodworking skills? No problem. I hadn't seen Don in years. His hair was as I remembered it, thick and rambunctious. He looked healthy despite being immobilized in his wheelchair. But his hands were the telltale, curled in unnaturally like the closed talons of a redtail or peregrine or … an owl.

Cameron pushed Don ahead. I followed. She gestured me toward the sofa, positioning Don's wheelchair near to me and then sat on a footrest at his feet. Everything about their elegant and understated house returns you to the land, underscores their love of this region: wooden beams and floors; exquisite bronzes of desert fauna; paintings of cattle drives or mountain vistas; Native American throws; walls of books on Central Oregon history, plants, geology; and everywhere photographs of Don and Cameron on various trips and desert expeditions, at Museum functions. She touched him on the arm often while I directed questions to her, engaged him in the conversation. "Donny, what do you think?" "Donny, is that the right date?" He'd sometimes lift his head, one eye partially closed, the other siting me in its crosshairs.

"Don is still the head of everything," Cameron stated, looking at him fondly.

"Are you Don?" I ask.

He studied me with one eye.

Cameron loaned me a three-ring binder containing background about the museum's evolution. Dog-eared clippings, programs, and photos stuck out the sides. Typed on a thin sliver of paper and slipped underneath the plastic cover of the binder was the phrase "The main thing is to keep your main thing your main thing." "That was always Donnie's mantra," said Cameron. "It's mine now too."

I don't go to church as often as my conscience and Episcopal upbringing would dictate. But on the Sunday after having met with Don and Cameron I went to the early service at Trinity Church in Bend. The liturgy and ritual is familiar to me, the service a form of coming home and, spiritually, in for a landing. Something about the meeting with Don, the deer in my yard, the sunny, glorious, champagne quality of this high desert morning—I felt inspired to go. When delivering the sermon Christy Close Erskine, Trinity's priest, doesn't stand behind the lectern. Instead, she stands in the aisle to better engage her congregation. "Good morning!" she said enthusiastically. "Good morning," we answered. She took in a breath and began. "The main thing is to keep the main thing the main thing..."

I don't know if you pay attention to this sort of coincidence, but I do. Close attention. To Don. To that phrase. To the magic and inexplicable nature of what occurs in our lives and when. The main thing. What is the main thing for each of us? Reflecting on the high desert, John McPhee stated: "Supreme overall is silence. Discounting the cry of an occasional bird, the wailing of a pack of coyotes, silence—a great spatial silence—is pure in the basin and range." That is what Don Kerr speaks now. He speaks the poetry, the purity, and the power of silence. When he addressed me with that singular gaze, stock-still, so silent, I was moved to ask him: "What can I do for you? What do you need? What do you want? Are you alright?" And that is exactly what Don Kerr would want me to ask, not on his behalf, but on the behalf of the high desert he loves so much.

# Looking Up to Low

NOT ALL THAT LONG AGO BEND'S DESCHUTES RIVER was nothing more than a cog in the machinery of the lumber mills, a holding pen for logs, a place to dump waste generated by the forest products industry with the added appeal that the river was also the repository for household sewage and in the winter prone to overflowing its banks when there was an ice jam. The only people who lived near its temperamental and defiled waters were people who couldn't afford to live anywhere else—the millworkers. Modest bungalows sprang up helter-skelter, cheek-by-jowl in close clutches along the river, with the grand houses of the lumber moguls on higher and drier elevations—a respectful distance from the river that wordlessly received the refuse of their fortune-building, and from the small homes of those who toiled on their behalf.

I now live on the banks of the Deschutes River as it flows through downtown Bend. When first built in the 1930s, my cottage joined the ranks of what were pejoratively referred to as mill shacks. Mine originally consisted of a small living room, kitchen, and two tiny bedrooms separated by a small bath. The house was positioned as far from the river and as close to the curb of the street as possible. That is, until someone came along in the 1990s and added a wing that frankly faced and embraced the river. What a difference a few decades make.

When searching for property along the river I noticed the one I bought wasn't the only one that turned its back to the Deschutes. All the former millworkers' houses did. It seems they tried to deny the river's existence as best they could, oriented their homes exclusively toward the street, toward the hilltops, toward the American Dream they believed was proffered to anyone who would work as hard as they did. The hundreds of families who migrated to Bend from the Midwest in the early 1900s, scarcely one generation removed from Scandinavia, shunned any association with what might symbolize lower class standing, including proximity to the river. If they had to build on its banks, the living and dining rooms eschewed a river view. Sheds or garages built of waste lumber and odd lots from the mills were the only construction close to the water. Even in downtown Bend, the storefronts turned a blind side to the river. Only within the last two decades do businesses openly acknowledge this waterway, only now is there discussion of replacing two large downtown parking lots that have a first-class view of the river with something more imaginative, more embracing of the glistening ribbon of water that is Bend's hallmark.

I grew up on the East coast near the Merrimack River. In the 1800s it was one of the great industrial rivers of the northeast, dumping ground for the considerable waste produced by huge textile mills built along its banks. Like the Deschutes, the Merrimack had few residences on or near its shores, other than the modest homes of the workers. The early textile mill owners and city fathers lived on the hilltops, looked down on the hardworking laborers and on the river that carried the toxic by-products of their pursuit of wealth out to sea. In developing countries now the same pattern holds true. The dramatic rivers that cascade through the towns and cities don't attract development; instead the houses of the wealthy are perched on hilltops, favoring

a view. Like the Deschutes River of old, rivers in Central and South
America, Africa, and Asia are still repositories for refuse and waste,
for sewage and pollutants. Beggars and homeless make their homes
there, not the rich. Low is not socially cool in emerging communities
or nations. Low-life, lowdown, lowbrow, lowly, low-minded. The
Spanish word *baja,* meaning low, is a derogatory term in Mexico. In
Native American culture, if someone came from downriver it meant
someone was from a lesser tribe. The high positioning of one's house
or teepee denoted social standing, wealth, and prestige.

But as the engine of the economy shifts to cleaner industry, as
regulations are enacted that protect rivers, waterways in many parts
of the United States are being prettied, cleaned up. It is desirable and
fashionable to live next to the water, and increasingly expensive. Old
canneries on harbors, textile mills and factories along rivers, and mill
houses in lumber towns are being restored as chic living spaces. Bend
is no exception.

With the end of storing raw pine logs in the river in the 1970s and
of stockpiles on its banks in 1994, the advent in 1986 of a city sewer,
and the razing of the mills themselves in 1995 (those sites now filled
with snazzy shops, movie theaters, and restaurants), the river went
from being shunned to being acceptable, and now, to being a highly
desirable address.

Today the Deschutes River is being reclaimed and beautified
with the planting of willow, cattail, and native marsh grasses along
its banks. Instead of logjams, bands jam the night away in two
amphitheaters set adjacent to the river. Strollers, with lattes in hand,
walk its banks. Mothers push prams. Joggers dash by in tight Lycra
suits. Couples paddle canoes lackadaisically on the flat water while
kayakers downstream run the white. Visitors scatter breadcrumbs to
the indulged ducks and geese that never leave. In winter, the young
and young at heart sled down a hill in Drake Park that ends thrillingly
at the edge of the river. In summer, they dive off footbridges, drift in
big black inner tubes, or frolic with inflated colorful sea monsters
at beaches created since the city lifted the ban on swimming in

1998. Stream flow and fish habitat are being improved. The Bend City Council has plans, if not the money, to dredge the silt that has accumulated in the river. The riverside banks that used to store thousands of board feet of logs have been cleared, creosote sins buried, and, in commemoration of Bend's centennial year in 2005, were dedicated as more riverside park area for Bend residents to enjoy.

Along the downtown run of the river, former mill houses are turning their remodeled and uplifted faces to the water, their owners paying a considerable sum for the privilege. These pint-sized homes are selling for close to a million dollars on river frontage of maybe twenty-five feet with prices holding, though sales slowing, during the recent recession. Suddenly the slow flow, the close in, the contemplative and, yes, the lowdown-ness, is something people seek. Not having to drive downtown is a value. High-density living has become less a socio-economic statement of need than a political one of responsibility as residents watch the land around them devoured by new construction. The chance to watch a blue heron successfully negotiate its long, lanky limbs onto the narrow branch of a willow; to see an osprey inscribe lazy circles in the sky as it scopes out its breakfast; or to spy the pair of bald eagles who call Drake Park home wing royally overhead—all the while within walking distance of shops and restaurants—is not a tough assignment. To be woken by the unharmonious and humorous chorus of ducks and geese, like irritated commuters wielding tiny air horns; to carefully negotiate boundary agreements between your river-fronting lawn and the nesting site of Trumpeter swan; or to see the head of the otter, like a brown tennis ball, as he floats past on his back, munching the crawdad held between his paws, are rare pleasures in a downtown setting.

As Bend grows, those subscribing to the top-of-the-heap theory have to drive farther and farther to get there. What they look down on now are their equals, their peers, as the economy reinvents and diversifies, as concerns about gas prices and sprawl prompt those who could own McMansions and McRanches to reconsider. No longer does higher necessarily mean wealth and power. Increasingly it means inconvenience. Bend's downtown is getting cozier and more livable, with lofts and apartments making an appearance in its core. The urban run of the Deschutes River is becoming more and more like a western version of a Venetian canal with neighbors crisscrossing in canoes and kayaks to have a barbecue with friends or to chew the proverbial fat over the gunnels of their watercraft instead of over a picket fence. These river-dweller snobs-in-reverse disdainfully dismiss the shouting, boastful, glistening mountain views and their pretense of permanence, preferring instead the meditative flow of water that reminds and reminds and reminds us just how ephemeral we are. It's a point being taken into thoughtful consideration by an increasing number, as evidenced by the booming demand for river views, lots, and homes. Anymore, river dwellers in downtown Bend are envied, yes, even looked up to.

# What One Thing

THE DINNER PARTY WAS HELD in an elegant private residence in Bend. The construction of the house was a feat of engineering, all fifty-five hundred square feet of it precariously balanced on a steep west-facing flank of Awbrey Butte. The home's brilliant green lawn, manicured garden, and man-made waterfall abutted snarls of dusky sagebrush and native juniper that grow in powdery volcanic high desert soil on an adjacent empty lot. Over hors d'oeuvres, a sultry jazz quartet wafting over the outdoor speakers, one of the guests asked what one thing each of us would create in Bend that we felt would contribute to ensuring it remained the place and community we loved. As I looked around, I imagined what the old-timers would have to say.

*Old-timer: Time was when Awbrey Butte was home only to sage and juniper, jackrabbit and bobcat, coyote and cougar. Elk migration lapped along the western edge. It wasn't much as a landmark. Nowhere near as high as Pilot Butte that guided wagon trains and their slack-jawed drivers looking for the river crossing at Farewell Bend in the 1800s.*

*Nothing for a cow to eat. No timber on it. Just scrub. Couldn't give it
away. Good for nothing. But turns out it could grow houses. Houses,
houses. Gradually began to work their way up the sides of the butte
like flood cycles—each wave of construction a new high-water mark in
population, folks with money, and the appetite for a fine view.*

We reflected on the question, seated on a deck with a panoramic
view of the Cascades, including the not-so-dormant South Sister, a
growing bulge of molten mystery on her west flank. The sunset was
psychedelic thanks to the scrim of smoke from the summer's spate of
forest fires, which had scorched thousands of acres of forests within
twenty miles of where we sat. As the night descended lights became
visible scattered across a nearby golf course community, and even
more lights in the direction of Shevlin Park, the pride of the city's
park system, which straddles the western edge of the beleaguered
urban growth boundary and is increasingly encroached on by
development. Before the 2009 recession, Bend was the sixth fastest
growing city in the United States. Though caught with its hand in
the building frenzy jar, Bend's housing market has stabilized. The
shocking unemployment rate of 15 percent, due to an excessive and
unwise dependence on construction, is improving. And people are
still coming here. Yesterday the population sign read 83,000. In 1995 it
said 29,425. Sitting on the deck we could hear traffic. There's nowhere
in town that isn't true now. I don't mean the intermittent sound of a
single car driving by, but a pervasive drone. It's probably commuters
headed home on the parkway, as Bend's labor force is increasingly
unable to afford to live in Bend.

*Old-timer: Before you could say biscuit, houses everywhere on
Awbrey. Houses the likes of which you've never seen. Bathrooms bigger
than my entire mill shack! Houses in places they shouldn't be, if you
want to know what I think—on sandy, unstable ground, hanging out
over the edge like that.*

In Bend there are more cars than people—evidenced by two-,
three-, and four-car garages on the new houses being constructed. The
way gas prices are headed, those garages will soon be the architectural

relic of a time we thought petroleum supplies would never end, a time we thought their consumption would not exhaust the health of this planet. The layer of haze visible when driving down from Mount Bachelor can't always be attributed to summer forest fires. All the houses and shopping malls and golf courses and roads—everything visible today in Bend has happened in the short space of one hundred years. How many times, because of the iconic fantasies we pin on the lapel of the American West, have we been seduced by the notion that we are in charge or that one thing or another is limitless? The view that night could easily have seduced us back into believing that was still the case, that there were still no limits.

*Old-timer: Desert is a harsh, dry place. Made women cry. Lonely and godforsaken. And yet the miracles folks today have created—making the desert look like an Eden, like they was God Himself.*

The varied answers to the evening's question—"What one thing?"—revealed our shared caring for the community as well as our different perspectives: an expanded regional and local public transit system, green belts separating Central Oregon communities, more job opportunities, a performing arts center, wage equity, a state highway bypassing Bend, affordable housing, free family planning and medical clinics, expansion of the urban growth boundary (UGB), no expansion of the UGB, more ethnic diversity (a *New York Times* article was referenced as saying that in Bend "diversity is defined by the color of your Subaru"), a four-year liberal arts college, wilderness and waterways protection.

The questioner and his wife had lived in Bend eleven years. They had retired early and moved permanently to the place they had previously only enjoyed on weekends and vacations. Their grown children now lived at various locations in the United States. You could tell this was a question he had asked at other, similar gatherings. You could tell he and his wife genuinely cared about the answers and that there was some likelihood they would put some of their resources to work for the ideas they favored most: medical care for the underserved and natural resource protection. They are just two among Bend's many modern-day Medicis who sustain and support Bend's social, cultural, and educational programs.

The area is home to an astounding number (four hundred) of nonprofits, which was why a dinner party just for the sake of informally bringing people together was such a pleasure. A good percentage of the social gatherings in Bend are fundraisers. We agreed the number of philanthropic organizations was symptomatic of the willingness of citizens in this community to rise to the challenge to do what the state, were it managing its affairs better, should be taking care of: social services, education and arts funding, even infrastructure improvements. Bend's system of roundabouts, each framing a piece of privately funded (sometimes controversial) public art, was conceived by Michael Hollern, CEO of the Brooks Resources Corporation and one of Bend's civic-minded and visionary developers.

We celebrated the heartening evidence that Bend's baton for leadership, philanthropy, and entrepreneurial chutzpah is being enthusiastically taken up by the twenty- and thirty-somethings. Not so many years ago there was real concern that the educated young would not return to Bend and that those choosing vocational careers could not make a living wage here. The lumber mills were the dominant economy but weren't hiring. Tourism-related jobs paid and still pay little. It wasn't clear what returning college grads would do for work that would challenge them and take advantage of their education. Even if they found employment, could the community rival the fun- and inspiration-factor of the cities where they had been educated or had held their first jobs? I don't of course mean physical recreation. Are you kidding? Surrounded by BLM land on the east and Forest Service acreage to the south and west, many days of sunshine, few days of rain, Bend is heaven for hikers, rock climbers, mountain and road bikers, golfers, skiers—you name it. (A visitor from New York, after eyeing the throngs of Lycra-clad runners, bicyclists, and kayakers churning through town remarked to me: "I couldn't possibly live here. I couldn't pass the physical.")

No, I mean recreation for the mind and spirit—the performing, visual, and literary arts, lecture series, great music. I mean raising Bend's level of discussion above, well, golf scores, the new boat or car, training programs indulged in by young bucks and geezer jocks alike (myself included in the latter category), wine cellars and clubs, the latest beauty treatment (more spas than restaurants in Bend), the last drive-by trip to Europe or Bali or Brazil. I have a friend who fashioned her own red, white, and blue campaign bumper sticker for the candidate Hugh Bris. She says most people in Bend ask her who Hugh Bris is and what he's running for. Few get the joke. There's a saying bantered about in Bend: "Stay here long enough and you get dumb and friendly." I have been here long enough to have a pretty good idea what it means. Living on this high desert island, it is easy to forget the rest of the world, to ascribe importance to the unimportant, to forget our relationship with the bigger picture. I mean I have nothing against fun—but pet parties? They are growing in popularity in Bend—where it's very possible there are more dogs than cars. I heard about a pet party held at an Awbrey Butte home for two- and four-legged friends complete with doggie party favors, "peticures," and games such as jump-through-the-hoop or catch-the-Frisbee. It wasn't clear if the two-legged guests got to compete or only the canines. Knowing Bend, probably both. As the dust from China's storms settles on the slopes of Mt. Bachelor, it is crucial we remember the causes and concerns of a wider world we have an obligation to care for.

*Old-timer: Fancy cars slip out from under them automatic garage doors, take on the off-road challenge of the drive to the grocery store, or maybe to the video shop to rent a movie about the Wild West, home to sagebrush and juniper, jackrabbits and bobcat, coyote and cougar. Don't get me started on the subject of pet parties. Used to be any dog worth its salt had a job to do—herding cattle and sheep. Now, they're all dolled up with bandanas and such tied around their necks.*

But the level of discussion *is* on the rise if the number of excellent social and conservation programs, cultural and arts events are any indication. In some ways the Bend Film Festival, founded in 2004 by thirty-something Katie Merritt, is as significant to the region as a young Don Kerr's idea to launch the High Desert Museum was a quarter of a century ago; Christine Winters and Robin Holdman as important in launching Volunteers In Medicine in 2001 as Sister Kathryn Hellman was to Saint Charles Hospital in the seventies; Deschutes Land Trust Director Brad Chalfant's effort to acquire thirty-three thousand acres of land west of Bend for recreation and wildlife as key as Bill Healy's creation of Mt. Bachelor Ski Resort as a young man in the sixties. Young go-getters such as Travis Yamada, thirty-two, who moved from California in 1992, recommend getting with the program, pitching in. "Be proactive," he urges. Yamada, the owner of a contracting business in Bend, dedicates his spare time to the creation of his urban answer to "what one thing": a series of skate parks ("decks") throughout the city, free for kids to use. As author and playwright Leonard Gross, who recently moved to Bend from San Francisco, stated, "Bend is a place that doesn't want anyone to fail."

*Old-timer: We came here to work. To homestead or fell trees or work in the mills. Came for the work. We hunted, put up the vegetables from our gardens. Can't make out what anyone does for a living anymore. I'll tell you what, I never thought I'd stand on the very spot where I gave thirty years of my working life and see a Victoria's Secret there now. Mills all gone. Farms too. It's like being preceded in death by a child. Unnatural."*

One of the couples who joined in on formulating an answer moved from California to Awbrey Butte with their young children only six months before—newcomers even by Bend's increasingly lax standards for long-timers. (Bend resident Claudia McDonald thinks Bend's motto should be "Veni, Vidi, Velcro.") He continues to commute to work in California each week, thankful for this summer's addition of a direct flight to Los Angeles from the growing Bend–Redmond airport, although he looks forward to being more virtual, accomplishing from a high-tech home office much of what he now travels to do.

His wife stays in Bend, jitneying their young family to soccer or swimming practice, music, dance, gymnastic, or language lessons. She reported her young son, shortly after their move, remarked that "there was so much nature here." His favorite place, she said, is the High Desert Museum where he can observe otters, porcupines, lynx, snakes, lizards. In point of fact, at the museum he is observing everything that used to flourish where he now lives, on Awbrey Butte—everything, that is, except for a cougar. There is no cougar on display at the High Desert Museum, although these beautiful cats undoubtedly roam its campus. I hope this boy will grow to know the museum is not the destination, but the gateway to an intimate relationship with the thing itself: this amazing high desert. I hope he will come to know absolutely that nature is not a theme park, but real, very real. (Recent drownings in the Deschutes River prompted one angry citizen to ask that city officials do something about the river, make it safer, despite the fact that the victim didn't know how to swim and didn't have on a life jacket when she headed downriver on an inner tube.)

*Old-timer: Mother nature. Keep an eye on her. She has a way of circling back around to remind just who is in charge. I'm not referring to that bulge on the flank of the South Sister, a bulge, should it get ornery, that could bury the town of Sisters. Damn well could. Or that pretty little Mirror Pond in the center of Bend filling up with silt, turning into a marsh right before our eyes. I'm not referring to the likelihood we're pumping the desert dry to take care of all the thirsty folks. Nope. I'm talking about the cougar on Awbrey Butte. Folks got pretty excited when the remains of a small dog were found, house cats came up missing. Forest Service folks investigated, decided it was the work of a cougar. Experts in cougar tracking called up. Men peered at the underbrush through binoculars out of their green government trucks. I speculate it might be the first time some of the folks living there looked up into the trees around their houses, took time to notice them, busy as they all seem to be. Could say that cougar forced them to return to a relationship with nature just for a spell. The cougar hasn't been caught. I have to say*

*I'm kinda glad. Did you know them cats lay claim to a territory of two hundred square miles or so? This one happened to include Awbrey Butte in its watch.*

What wakes each of us up is unique, but wake up we must, collectively and individually. In Bend we live close to nature. Like everyone everywhere we have insulted her in ways small and large. But given our proximity to Oregon's outback it's just possible we are more readily and quickly made aware of the magnitude of the insult. If we're lucky, the delay time is less here, the high desert environment less forgiving, less tolerant, less patient. Pick up a fistful of the dry desert dirt, hike through the Ponderosa, learn to identify what flies, what grows, what the rocks instruct. All combine to remind us we weren't first to this place. Imposing our will on the West has to give way to something else.

What one thing would each of us create in Bend that we felt would contribute to keeping it the place we loved and make it even better? It's a question that both humbles and inspires me. Humbles because I remember when I thought everything was possible, including being in control, when I believed humans had all the answers. And inspires because I now know so much of what must be done has to do with paying attention in ways I never did before, to the ebb and flow, the high and low tide of land, sky, water, and people as they migrate in and through their lives and landscapes.

My one thing? After dinner we walked back out to the deck under the obsidian night. A stocking cap of snow on the Cascades shone in the moonlight. We leaned over the prow of railing that jutted dramatically over the steep slope of Awbrey Butte and gazed out. The American West used to beckon us to come to the precipitous edge of man's claim and urge us to tame more, saddle-break more. Now the call of the American West is to shore up that collapsing edge, to protect and reclaim the wildness, and to knit ourselves together in the effort. We looked out at an environment, a place, a community we loved, knew we had to care for and nourish, not conquer and control, one that requires thoughtful attention—to its people, newcomers and old-timers, rich and poor; to its environment; to its unique expression. It was time to remove our earphones and listen to the song and language of the place itself. That's my one thing: help create listeners.

# Take A River
## Bend, Oregon 1905 – 2005

Listen from right here:
the muted falls, the night hawk's
call, an isolated quack, the heart's
skip, lap of paddle, the whisper
of wind through the quiet
colored end of evening.

Here in Bend, tonight,
said Bulletin publisher
George Putnam in 1913,
we envy no one.
He is still right.

Take a river and bend it,
a dream and transcend it.
Take adventure and seek it,
an idea and build it. January

1905. In light and city years,
Bend, you're so young. Stop
for a moment to run a finger
along the dusty shelf of history,
step in the footprint of cork
boot, leather brogan, beaded
moccasin to see where we
have been, where we might go.

*Ta-ma-no-hus chuck*, this magical river.
*Skoo-kum sagh-a-lie ill-a-hee*: mighty mountains.
*To-ke-tie*: so pretty. *Pol-ak-lie*: this night.

Chief Chinook, Chief Paulina, you fished
along this heron-priested shore, hunted
deer and elk on stealthy feet. Did you
not see the greed of trappers reaping
a Deschutes fat with fish and beaver?
Did you not hear the alarm of ox-cart
wheels? Homesteaders, thousands,
crossed a continent in wagons and carts
for land that is one third rock; for a chance
to stake their claim to hope, pulled
behind horse-drawn plow and rake.
Farewell Bend, Thomas Clark named it in 1851.
A place for these prairie schooners to port,
to clear land for dreams, to write ambition
in thin, blue flumes of river water Alexander
Drake channeled across this dry land.

Life then hard on proper women. Canned all
scorching summer over woodstoves. Tended
children, milk cow, garden, bonnet brims blown
backward by thirsty wind. They'd lift their skirts

to dodge dirt or boardwalk splinter; never showed
more than two inches of ankle; never walked
on Greenwood and Bond—especially when buckaroos
or herders tangled through town, chasing down sheep,
driving cattle through the streets. It was said
the dust didn't settle for days. When it did
the ladies of the night paid cash for their new shoes.

Bend, an outpost of hope, from range through world wars.
Before 1911 was the biggest empty in the whole country
with no railroad. Shaniko as far as you could go. From
there a wagon-road south, nothing but rut-holes and boulders.
Passengers would lay hold to help push Cornett coaches
stuck in a bog. Seven hours to Bend on a good day.

These same downtown streets platted according to wagon
widths: Bond and Wall three across, Oregon and Minnesota
only two. Folks scrambled for seats on the rickety stage,
heady with the sense of going to…who knew?

Oh, the intoxication of: "Who knew?" Who knew
what lay amid sleeping volcano, high prairie
and bright water that traced the shores of this high
desert island adrift in Central Oregon's starry deep.

The same year, 1910, that Bend first turned on a light,
captured the electrical might of the river, Harriman
and Hill drove the golden spike, opened wide Oregon's
trunk. Remember how the hiss and steam of locomotives
scared horses and kids silly? No sooner that iron road
laid down than lumber mills rumbled in its wake.
On your mark, Shevlin Hixon! Get set, Brooks Scanlon!
On go! they felled and skidded red-chested logs out
of forgiving forests. Down the Deschutes they rogued

and jammed. 1915—Bend, a timber town. Stirred
its coffee with its thumb! Ring up on the party line
and tell everyone! The men of Bemidji and Bowstring
heard the call. Loaded their families to hob and nail,

cut and trim a better life for all of them. The din of cars
and buggies crowded the widening reach of streets
and homes. Deals were made on the porch of Pilot
Butte Inn. The glow of Mill A's wigwam lit the pitch
boats of young boys' dreams. And their fathers sang
into every day, certain their loggin' woods life was here to stay.

Bend was booming. Hooray and fireworks! In '33
the town celebrated with Parades of Progress. Queens
of beauty floated by, seated on the backs of papier
swan, reflected in the blackened, nighttime pond.

Oh logger, oh planer, oh sawyer did you not hear
the alarm in the mill's whistle? Heed the cry
of the owl? In '94 the last log was sawed
and trimmed, wooden basilicas all torn red
down, save three smoke stacks that reach
straight up into the eye of the sky.
Boardwalks to sidewalks, sagebrush
to lavish scape. Good-bye Masterson Hardware,
hello high-end St. Clair Place. Old mill to new,
feast, fest, on the run. Efficiency, top
of the line, doctors and strong medicine.
Pole, pedal, paddle; person, place and thing.
Start and finish strong, right here in Bend.
A newly branded land rush is on! Now
houses, now condos, now centers of learning,
now land trust, now music, now film and writing.

Celebrate invention, amazement, and derring-do.
Harvest sun, snow and all things virtual. Bend
beckons us to regale on a cornucopia sublime
during this our allotted capsule of time.

But where now is the uncharted territory? Where
is the next land of "who knew"? What cries do we
fail to heed, alarms to hear as molten dreams shift
the sleep of the South Sister? Are we more river
than rock? More transient than not? Bend 2105.
The Indian chief would advise: Find four roads
that run side by side and choose the middle
one. Learn to see, eyes shut, with blinding sight.

We are writing the early pages of that spacious
and distant answer. It's a lot with a view thanks
to you: Fremont, Todd, Reid, Putnam, Ogden,
Eades, Egg and Drake; Sisemore, Overturf,
Sather and don't forget folks like Ruth Stover
and her square piano, her husband Dutch, and his
snappy banjo. Thank you for showing us how
to take a dream and transcend it, adventure
and seek it, an idea and build it;
to take a river and bend it,
to take a river and wend it
deep in our hearts.

# Highest Best Use

I SPENT TWO DECADES RANCHING in Central Oregon's High Desert. My then-husband, children, and I would be there still except that his methamphetamine addiction forced other outcomes. Maybe something else would have hooked him, dragged him through a self-made hell, prompted him to devastate his family, and ultimately, to take his own life if meth hadn't been available, but it was—readily available.

I can remember summer days on the ranch spent moving cattle off Twelve Mile Flat, cooking dinner for ten to fifteen ranch hands and guests, team-roping until dusk in the arena we built near the house. I'd read stories to my sleepy children, their hair slicked smooth after a bedtime bath, tuck them in. Then, grateful for a moment to myself, I'd go outside and lie on my back on the grass and listen to the sounds of the desert settling in. The sunset was like middle earth, its light so radiant. The Cascades in the distance were like black tusks in silhouette. Our lawn was separated from the irrigated hay meadows and the endless expanse beyond by a split rail fence that zigged its way around our irregularly shaped yard. I looked up into the giant black tarpaulin, tiny punctures of light growing brighter and brighter as the sun gave up its hold, night's dizzying carnival. I was at once made to feel bigger and smaller by the vastness—earth and sky—equally unfathomable, and, from my vantage point lying on the grass, equally as unpeopled. The Milky Way hovered soupy over the sleeping sage hills. The call of the coyote marked the parameters of encroaching darkness. My meditation might be interrupted by the distant growl of a low flying aircraft moving stealthily across the velvet dark, but nothing more.

This high desert suited me, my propensity to gaze and ponder, analyze and think. To be still. Ranch life suited my inclination to fall into line with the dictates of nature, harvest and birth repeated over and over again. To live a life that rewarded caring, adventure, courage and required humor, patience, and humility. The high desert doesn't have the postcard appeal of Moab, the Grand Canyon. Because of managing to stay off the front page of destination magazines, it affords quiet, isolation, and peace. I am certain, and it matters to me, I can claim to have walked where no one has walked before, been the first to discover a teepee ring of stones circling the campsite of nomadic Paiute tribes cycling through a century ago, initials carved in the bark of a juniper marking the passing of a covered wagon looking for the promised land. As they discovered, it wasn't here. The high desert sent many homesteaders away discouraged that nothing would grow, bedeviled by the wind, the cold, the dust.

After the last offer in 1909, the government took back the land the homesteaders didn't want. Over the years of administering those lands, the BLM developed a system for permitting various users on public lands. They referred to it as "highest best use." If barren land, with no pressure from recreational groups or environmentalists, it was generally offered to ranchers. Many ranches were bought and sold on the strength and size of their government lease. The BLM used the quaint and now outdated measure of "animal unit month," or AUMs, to calculate how many acres of public land it would take to carry a cow and her calf for one month, twelve times that needed to carry her for a year. In the sparse high desert an animal unit required more land than on almost any other area of public lands in the West.

Now, with increased demand on land from a wide variety of sources, all possible uses are given careful scrutiny. The process is an imperfect one, swayed by greater or lesser pressure from environmentalists, recreationalists, and ranchers. Over the past decade, two new and ironically contradictory "highest best uses" have emerged. I know about both.

Because of the perceived sense of promise of the open spaces, wilderness therapy programs have sprung up all over the West, taking kids with behavioral and/or drug issues into the outback to find their inner truths. Wilderness as therapy. The notion that land can fix a kid. It sells. I bought in, enrolling two of my children in such programs when substances threatened to become the organizing principle of their young, disrupted lives. Did it help them? I think so. But I don't know so. Would I do it again?

Hundreds of these programs have opened in Montana, Idaho, Oregon, and California since 1990. In Oregon alone there are thirty. Bend is the home base for six accessing a high desert area that encompasses one-fifth of the United States.

The Oregon legislature has wrestled with how to evaluate and regulate these programs that cater to kids who have lost their grip and sense of place, throwing them hard at the rugged outdoors to discover it and themselves again. Because there has been fallout. A few years ago two kids ran away from a program and held up an elderly ranch couple. In another, a staff member tried to subdue a belligerent young man who was threatening to do harm to himself and in the process the young man suffocated and died. Most recently, Mt. Bachelor Academy outside of Prineville, Oregon, closed due to allegations of abusive and strong-arm techniques used in trying to turn kids around. Critics say the notion of detoxing kids in extreme outdoor conditions is dangerous, cruel, and traumatizing. For parents, in addition to the gut-wrenching decision to pursue such a course of action, it's an expensive proposition. Wilderness therapy programs run anywhere from $7,000 to $15,000. Residential programs are a whole other, more expensive story. But given the desperate condition most of these adolescents are in when they arrive, the statistics are encouraging overall. The turnarounds are happening. The desert is delivering. And yes, under the circumstances, I would do it again.

Lying on my back, gazing at the stars on those summer nights at the ranch, the low flying aircraft I heard—though I didn't know it at the time—was as likely as not the Central Oregon Drug Enforcement team (CODE), their ultraviolet cameras scanning the range to pick up the heat generated from the night-burning methamphetamine labs hidden in the big, open desert. Invert the nighttime obsidian sky and there are constellations of a different sort: lights radiating from illegitimate meth kitchens set up in secluded corners of the desert attended by their skilled chefs. Maybe you've seen these chefs and not realized it. They stand outside, regardless of the temperature, jittery, smoking, not daring to go inside with a lit cigarette—might just as well throw it into a bucket of gasoline.

Smaller labs are set up everywhere, anywhere. After I had moved off the desert into Bend, two men rented a small bungalow behind my backyard fence. My house faced an upscale street; however, those behind mine faced a larger thoroughfare and ran the gamut of respectable to shabby. I was woken one night by the sound of snarling dogs. Peering through my bedroom curtain I saw the men hoisting over a branch of a tree in their yard what appeared to be a large piece of meat hung from a rope just out of the reach of two dogs. One man tormented the dogs, repeatedly kicking them, inciting them to turn savagely on one another, laughing wickedly. The other raised and lowered the rope, looking anxiously into the open door to the brightly lit kitchen, repeatedly reminded not to go inside by his dog-torturing friend. "Not while it's cookin.'"

I didn't turn them in. I didn't dare. I felt they might guess who squealed. Might come after me. I was persuaded the world conspired against me. Drugs had penetrated and contaminated every aspect of my life. I was still in the throes of having escaped my marriage, my own drug-induced nightmare, and this midnight vision—in town, adjacent to my newfound home, which I so desperately wanted to believe was safe from all this madness—paralyzed me in fear.

Labs so blatantly located are shockingly commonplace; however, setting up in the isolated areas near rural ranch and farm communities is more common, as it gives larger-scale meth producers access to the one chemical they need most—anhydrous ammonia, contained in farm fertilizer. Rural hardware stores sell acetone, Coleman fuel, charcoal lighter fluid—some of the other ingredients used to manufacture this addictive cocktail. It is sometimes called a blue-collar drug because it is so easy and cheap to make. It is a synthetic stimulant that can, in small quantities, be made in a portable cooler with ingredients bought at the corner drugstore despite efforts to regulate sales—ingredients like paint store solvent, lithium batteries, Sudafed, ephedrine from sinus medication. The stuff of simple cold remedies combined in a lethal stew and sold in a form that can be snorted, smoked, or injected. The consumer of meth is blue and white collar, male and female, and all races and ages (yes, parents, starting in middle school). The drug reputedly makes the user feel all-powerful, confident, sexy. As it does, it wastes away brain cells, wastes away families, wastes away the environment, producing six pounds of toxic waste for every pound of meth produced. The chemical by-products of meth labs have become one of the biggest environmental problems in the Central Oregon region. Officials from the DEQ are called out in their moon suits to clean up abandoned labs—acid, flammable solvents, sodium hydroxide, ammonia, pressurized cylinders and, a cultural irony, remnants of Martha Stewart sheets, preferred for straining chemicals thanks to their high thread count. When not attended to, the toxins remain active for decades. The number of labs seized in Deschutes County jumps exponentially each year. And they're not just out in the desert. They're next door in the seven-thousand-square-foot vacation rental, in the vacant apartment, in the double-wide.

Highway 97, which intersects Bend, Oregon, and arcs through the high desert, is officially recognized as a drug corridor, from Mexico, through California, and on to Canada. In 1999 Deschutes and Jefferson counties qualified as a High Incidence Drug Trafficking Area (HIDA) and were auspiciously honored with additional federal monies to fund the Central Oregon Drug Enforcement team. CODE had operated informally since 1989 until HIDA funding allowed the formalization of the program. Bob Smit, a retired veteran with the State Police, explained the growing presence of meth in eastern Oregon this way: "There is a hydraulic factor at work. Authorities squeezed the I-5 corridor in the late eighties so the labs moved east. In addition, the usage and therefore the demand for production increased dramatically." Driving along Highway 97, there are countless dirt roads that veer off into the desert. I'd wager the chances are good that the van loaded with kids on the first week of their three-week rehabilitation crosses a road that leads farther out to a secluded lab. I'd wager the meth producers track those vans with their high-powered binoculars to make sure there are no chance encounters.

"Highest, best use." Thanks to the sullen vagaries of our social appetites, the warring highest best uses of the high desert are drug production and drug rehab. Oregon's outback is mimicking the rest of the country—production and rehabilitation, trafficking and enforcement. Is this as good as it gets? I have always relied on the desert for answers. Maybe the answer isn't to be found there anymore. Maybe our instinct to self-destruct is going to overwhelm even the best possible promises, the best possible uses.

# A Tribute to Van and Helen Houston

THE POEM THAT FOLLOWS IS A TRIBUTE to two Central Oregonians, Van and Helen Houston of Prineville. In addition to being a trapper in the great tradition of this ancient form of hunting, Van was also our mailman, delivering mail three times a week on the South Fork, making his way in "the stage," as we referred to his truck, along Roberts Route, past the Prineville reservoir, along Camp Creek, a round trip drive of 130 miles. Our mailbox, a wooden box on legs with a crudely fashioned door and our brand, Rafter Q, painted on the side, was his last stop. He not only delivered mail but also transported houseguests who had gotten as far as Prineville on the bus from Portland, or baby chickens we ordered from catalogues each spring. On the return trip he once delivered a urine sample to the doctor's office to confirm what I had guessed: I was pregnant.

He tanned and stretched and cured a tiny moleskin hide for my firstborn's dollhouse. He was a self-proclaimed "desert rat," his family having settled there in the 1900s, and thanks to his keen eye and inquisitive mind, he was an authority on the desert and an amateur historian, spotting and recording signs of the Meeks Cut-off trail and evidence left by later settlers traveling through that part of the desert. As a young man he worked for Bill Brown (see "Morally Certain") as a "sheep licker," as those who helped with lambing were called.

After she retired from teaching in the Crook County schools, Helen traveled with Van in their camper, setting up in the desert for the winter while he trapped, returning to town every so often for supplies. She was the mistress of her kitchen and a craftswoman—knitting and crocheting, sewing and doing macramé, dignifying every traditional homemaker's activity by her exquisite attention and skill. If either of them were five feet tall I'd be surprised. They had a deep affection for the high desert and for one another.

I followed two different trappers with my camera when I lived in the desert, developing the images in the darkroom I set up in the ranch bunkhouse. Spending time with Van, I came to appreciate the ancient art of trapping, his respect for his prey, his conscientiousness in checking his lines. I endured the top-secret and God-awful stench of his trap bait, made from rotten rattlesnake meat. When I show my photographs from those winters they are judged offensive, cruel. Yet his was an old and time-honored trade, one that had rules and traditions that Van observed to the letter. He always said that he felt he and the coyote were equally and fairly matched. He didn't trap bobcat because he felt he had the upper hand given their innocent curiosity. Everything in moderation. If Van and Helen were king and queen of the world, we would take modestly and give generously.

# Trapping Coyotes

For years I was the only trapper
running lines from Prineville to Suplee.
Checked all fifty miles every three days.
Got around in my old Willy's Jeep.
Hell of a rig.

Seems like we'd get in a different
fix every day. Never gave it much
thought back then, like that bridge that gave way,
me and Willy only half across.
Hell of a rig.

The wife would stay in the house trailer.
We'd haul it out middle November
when their fur's starting to set up good.
Park it at one ranch or another.
Day after day

she'd stay happy putting up preserves
or knitting sweaters for the grandkids.
We'll have been married fifty years June.
My Helen, she is quite the Helen,
day after day.

Ranch folk were happy to see us come
set out traps for the sons of a gun.
Coyotes was hard on new calves and leps.
Packs of seven gang up and take them,
you darn betcha.

And one thing about the sneaky Pete,
it's an even match. Not to boast, but
he's that smart. Fooled me often as not.
A finer thinker I'd like to meet.
You darn betcha.

We'd spend the winter in the desert.
If the weather got too ornery, then
Helen and I'd stretch and cure the hides,
otherwise I was running them lines,
chasing coyotes.

I'd mix the scent the summer before.
Came up with a perfect concoction.
The main ingredient was rattler. Yep.
Snake meat—minced and rank. Just right for
chasing coyotes.

Setting the traps is quite a to-do.
Find their spot marked with scat, dig a hole.
Bury the contraption, then cover it
with twigs—careful not to spring the thing.
No sirree Bob!

Spread the scent around. Hell, I soaked my
clothes in it. Any trace of human
smell, you just as well quit. Last off, sweep
up your tracks with a juniper bough,
yes sirree Bob!

Time or two I'd snag one, foot mangled
in the trap, fur straight up on his back.
I'd wave my hammer up and down slow.
His yellow eyes watched my every move,
like so, like so.

Then whack! I'd smack him right on the nose.
stunning him good, I'd stand on his throat,
to cut off his air, and watch his mouth
open and close, his feet moving fast,
like so, like so,

in a dead run, as he breathed his last.
Some get lazy and shoot the buzzard.
Not me. I'm paid premium for hides
with no holes. Worth the extra effort,
I do suppose.

When finally he'd give up the ghost
I'd say thanks, my turn to get lucky.
His time will come 'round next, most likely.
A person can never know such things,
I don't suppose.

Day would come to take the hides to town.
Ten stacks, twenty each, tied up in twine.
Fur buyers would come in the spring,
gather there at the Powell Butte Grange.
Gosh darnedest thing.

These men in suits come up from L.A.
to wheel and deal with the likes of me.
I made a good profit on each and every pelt.
Gosh darnedest thing,

just to think of them hides trimmed and sewn
together to be worn by fancy
folks down yonder. Did make me stop and
wonder why all the fuss and bother.
All's the better,

if I get to match wits with the whelp,
see some good country, help the rancher,
put white bread on my Helen's table,
and get someone a fine fur as well.
All's the better.

# Cows Kill Salmon

THE FIRST "COWS KILL SALMON" BUMPER STICKER I saw was on the dented tailgate of a puny pickup in Bend. I was in town loading the giant bed of our 4x4 Dodge with valves, hoses, belts, swather parts, sacks of chicken feed, vaccines for the upcoming days of processing hundreds of mother cows. I was filling our truck with muscle and brawn and can-do, with coolers full and paper bags stuffed with groceries to last a month. Then the two-hour return trip back to the ranch. "Get a clue!" I muttered. "How stupid is that? What does that guy know about getting food on the table? Nothing, that's what."

The pickup belonged to Bill Marlett, the founder of the Oregon Natural Desert Association and the author and originator of the "Cows Kill Salmon" slogan and campaign. I wouldn't know that or meet him for years. But I did know one thing. Whoever he was, with a bumper sticker like that, he was the enemy. What he stood for challenged a way of life I had embraced completely.

Oppositional thinking makes everything less complicated. I am this not that, believe this not that. They are not this and so I am not one of them. Without good fences it's not possible to have good neighbors. What, all just sit around compromising all the time? Doesn't friction create the sparks to fire new inventions? Provide the flint of new ideas? I my way'd or the highway'd out of town, back to the desert, back to the large-scale, ranching way of the chosen few.

In case you didn't know, ranching *is* the ultimate. It's the dream. It matters. It is the way of right life. Everything else is silly in comparison. Ranchers are artists, inventors, bankers, businessmen, hydrologists, farmers. They know what hard work is. They stay up all the long night swathing hay or calving first calf heifers, then spend all the sweltering day horseback or all the sub-zero day tossing hay to rime-covered cows. Ranchers learn to dance with the seasons, to honor traditions, to speak the language of the drover.

Ranching has its own humor. Take income: "Psychic, mostly." That's what our neighbor used to say. Or on the day calves are sold and shipped, the annual payday: "If you keep weighing them, they don't get any heavier," the wry comment from the cattle buyer, his pen poised. The anthem is: Country is good, city is evil. The refrain: Where a man's a man and sacks are made of burlap. No small gestures. No small checks. No small measures. Broad brush, big tractors, big ideas, big pivots deep-knee bending across the fields, sending geysers of water into the air. Big risk. "Gonna be a bear, be a grizzly." And what could be more picturesque? The cowboy's white shirt filling with the summer's evening breeze as he lopes home, cows lowing to their calves, emerald meadows as the shadows grow long, stout and shiny buckskin and sorrel quarter horses held in the corral for tomorrow's long drive to higher pasture, saddles hanging in the cathedral-sized red barn, ropes, halters, and bridles waiting, tidy on their nails.

What could feel more powerful than owning land, lots of it, or more self-sufficient than a shotgun still warm from shooting pheasant and chukar on your own spread, pulling small rainbow trout from your own creeks, making your own antelope sausage, collecting eggs from your own chickens, apples from your own orchard? Or the satisfaction of introducing the land to its greater capacity and purpose, plowing up the soil, planting crops, delivering water to places that had been dry for centuries? What greater sense of accomplishment than managing the migration of thousands of cattle with miles of wire, enhancing their productivity with artificial insemination or specially enhanced feed and growth supplements. Rancher as conductor, nature the compliant orchestra.

Then I moved into town. I went from living on hundreds of thousands of unpopulated acres to living cheek-by-jowl on a crowded street. My children were wide-eyed and wary. Me too, as I surveyed the frontier of single parenting, of going to an office every day, of single-handedly supporting three children. My son rigged an orange juice can on a string so he could talk house-to-house to the girl next door. We lived that close. My oldest daughter walked downtown to meet friends and go to a movie in three minutes. That close. I remember coaching myself not to hog-call my children to dinner. The neighbors could hear. This was a far cry from the then-manager of the GI Ranch, Art Foss, telling me: "Miss Ellie, you're the nicest neighbor I have." My reply: "I am the *only* neighbor you have and I am ten miles from your front door. But I'll take it as a compliment."

The ebb and flow of life in town was punctuated by trash collection day, lawn or snow removal services, not by brandings, gathering cattle, baling hay. The only weather-related concerns pertained to ski or golf conditions, not a crop-crushing hailstorm or so much snow you couldn't get to the cattle to feed them or a misty, persistent spring rain that would make the grass jump.

It took moving "in" for me to truly and fundamentally appreciate the "out." It took living a dramatically compressed life to finally knowing, at a cellular level, what an expansive, fragile, drop-dead gorgeous beauty the high desert is. I began to pay attention to how little attention I had paid, to how little attention was being paid. I had been a trespasser in the desert: presumptive, arrogant, willful. I read in Bend's paper about the tireless and often maligned defenders of urban river trails, the Deschutes River, the Badlands on Bend's outskirts, the Hart Mountain Antelope Refuge. As resort communities were built pell-mell, I could swear I heard the sound of a pebble rattling in the empty lava canyons of the drained subterranean aquifers. I saw the panting fish in the slack waters of the Middle Deschutes and reflected on the eroded banks of Camp Creek that ran through our desert ranch. Did cattle in fact kill streamside plants as Bill Marlett's campaign maintained? Did the silt cattle created really suffocate the insects the fish feed on? Did the degraded streams become broader, more shallow, too warm for fish? Where had the rainbow trout that used to inhabit Camp Creek gone?

These questions insisted their way into my workday in the office seated at my computer, or fixing dinner for my children. As I made grocery lists, helped with homework, tended our urban menagerie of gerbils, a parakeet, dog, and cat, the headlines about the effects of hormones in meat jumped out at me. What was the small white pill we had injected subcutaneously in the calves' ears? What was the toxic chemical we poured along the spine of the cow's back? What was in the numerous vaccines and boluses we administered? In the chicken feed? I was ashamed I didn't know. This was when I started to ask myself: "Had I really been part of something perfectly beautiful?"

When I met Bill Marlett I found him to be, ironically, very like the stereotypical rancher, with a kind of owning-it-all stance and manner, a stare-down demeanor, strong, capable hands, his worn jeans and work shirt a matter of functionality, not fashion. A too-much-work-to-do, urgent energy seemed to push him from inside. He moved to Bend from his native Wisconsin in 1984 to fight plans for hydroelectric installations on the Deschutes River. He won, winning the Deschutes a state scenic waterway designation, a cause he went on to champion on behalf of dozens of Oregon rivers. He founded Bend's Environmental Center and made the Oregon Natural Desert Association one of the most effective grassroots organizations in the West, if not the nation. Its aim? To end grazing on public lands. Altogether. Zero, zip, nada.

Does he or those championing similar causes have no choice but to aim for the extreme to win a partial solution? Is that the only way? Does it take revolution to regain some sort of tolerable middle ground? Greenpeace folks used to be regarded as a bunch of extremists. Al Gore won a Nobel Peace Prize for many of the same messages. Do we have to push against each other to know who we are and who the other is? Can we invent, improve, progress without being in opposition?

We are woefully clumsy creatures, even when well intended, even when we think we are on the side of "right." Oregon Public Broadcasting recently aired a series to invoke the beauty of the high desert. One episode filled the TV screen with a herd of pronghorn running across a desert flat. The shot was taken from a helicopter, the noisy rotors churning just above the terrified animals. The shot went on and on with classical music enhancing the image of freedom and beauty and wildness. After awhile the antelope's tongues were hanging out, the terrified herd turning, twisting, stumbling, some falling. This was a portrait of panic, not beauty extolled. In an effort to invoke custodial caring the good people of OPB did harm. Man's predilection for instructing, doing "good," according only to his terms, is shocking.

But there are hopeful signs. Ranchers are reclaiming native grasses using innovative grazing practices, are diverting cattle away from streams to transportable troughs powered by solar panels, are producing hormone-free, natural beef, and implementing costly best practices despite rising production costs across the board. Reclamation efforts on the 278,000 acres of the Hart Mountain National Antelope Refuge has fish returning to spawn in creeks, streams crazy with growth and flourishing native flora and fauna. And some of the many ranchers who have been using right, sustainable practices all along are finally being recognized.

At an annual formal dinner in Portland, Oregon, The High Desert Museum recognizes stewards of the high desert. This particular year Doc and Connie Hatfield, well known in the region for their decades of thoughtful and scientific range management practices and for the creation of a consortium of ranches raising organic beef, were to be honored. They seemed to sit in watchful silence, as though, in observing the urban noise and self-importance, the oppositional thinking, they wordlessly and wistfully acknowledged that the chances of enough people truly getting to know and care about the land were slim. They sat there taking in all the fanfare and hubbub, as though their ears were pressed against a shell that cried and whispered of how catastrophic this lack of profound and genuine understanding would be.

"Honey, get the gate." That's what my former husband would say to me, and I would. Happily. He'd pull the pickup on through, I'd shut the gate behind, and we'd drive through the vast corridors of our land, surveying on a golden evening mothers paired up happily, fresh brands on the flanks of the calves. Traversing the meadow, I'd lean out the truck window breathing in the sage-scented air.

I now have an equal interest in pulling fences as opening and closing them. I now realize that, unlike the many conscientious and best-practice ranchers, I sailed in a prairie schooner but never looked deep into the ocean. I don't advocate jamming things into reverse. I don't suggest eliminating cattle or cowboy, green collar or blue. I do suggest that the oppositional thinking we seem to require be shifted in concept. That we oppose bad practice, not each other, see land both as a means and an end, develop prescription lenses that work for both the entrepreneurial and the custodial vision.

"Cows kill salmon." When I first saw that bumper sticker I pictured a big-bellied Hereford mother cow standing streamside, her front hoof planted on a writhing salmon while she distractedly chewed her cud, gazing off into nothingness in that vapid, bovine way. But really all it means is that we are intricately and beautifully and dangerously connected.

# Two Alices

THERE ARE MORE WOMEN LIVING ON THEIR OWN in the United States now than at any time in the history of this country. Historically wars drove this statistic—the Revolutionary War, the world wars—leaving countless widows. Now it is chalked up to a variety of circumstantial causes. Of interest to me, because I am one of them, are the legions of middle-aged, middle-class women in the United States who find themselves on their own because a relationship has failed or eluded them.

What this means sociologically or anthropologically I don't venture to guess. But, to state the obvious, being alone as a middle-aged woman takes skills not required when living with a man or companion, where two minds, and incomes, and two sets of eyes and muscles, can weigh in on the issues of the day. I have to think about maintaining my car and yard, furnace and fridge, paying the bills and balancing my budget all on my own. I stay involved, informed, and active so as not to become brittle in my opinions, the result of holding debates only with self. I try to dodge the fear-based thinking directed at older single women by our culture: the uncertainty of my physical and financial future, the incantations to be old, act old, go away, live assisted.

Married or single requires some loss of wingspan. On her own, a woman learns to trust herself, use her wits, but in the end the size of her life canvas is diminished by going it alone. Conversely, though secure with a husband to take care of her, the dependent woman's figure-it-out skills often atrophy. Will she ever fully know what she is capable of on her own? Many single women are surprised to find the pleasure they derive in designing a life, their life. Of course there are days when I long for a male companion and lover who sits next to me. We lean into each other. He holds my hand and we stare out at the same figurative point on the same metaphorical horizon. But the shocking amount of energy women, me included, squander on waiting, looking for the perfect mate could light up Las Vegas or, at the very least, be used more productively.

You won't be surprised that I turned to the high desert for some answers, seeking out two Alices who had each ranched on her own in overlapping lives.

I sensed they would be able to give me some tips on being a woman on my own. In some striking ways, they each represent aspects of myself, which made this musing all the more engaging. One, a writer—serious, analytical, well educated, and resigned to never finding a male partner. The other—impulsive, spontaneous, even reckless, enjoyed the opposite sex but was just as happy on her own. Alice Day Pratt suffered the prejudice many felt toward a single woman doing a "man's" work. Alice DeLore dared anyone to express such a notion in her presence.

## *Alice Day Pratt (1872–1963)*

In the early 1980s, ranching on the South Fork of the Crooked River with my family, I was lucky to meet Brooks Ragen, an historian by avocation who loved the high desert. He chose a history topic each year to research. One project landed in his lap—or rather under his feet, for beneath the floorboards of a cabin adjacent to property he acquired in Post, he found journals written by Alice Day Pratt who, it turned out, homesteaded there as a single woman starting in 1912. I was writing daily then, between chores and children, and remember being intrigued by the idea of a woman going it alone only a few decades before and a few miles from where I was seated at my desk, and thankful I would never have to. I never dreamt I would return to her pages as a single woman in search of guidance.

Born to well-educated and well-off easterners, her family moved west due to Mr. Pratt's health issues and need for a drier climate, settling in a secluded Black Hills canyon fifteen miles from Rapid City, South Dakota, in 1886. It is there Alice Day Pratt's love of living in a remote location took hold.

For a number of years she worked as a teacher in North Carolina and Arkansas. But at age thirty-eight Alice Day longed for what the South Dakota years had offered, to "build a farm, whereon I could exercise my delight in all forms of nature life…." She had also come to terms with being single. "About the year nineteen-ten came to me—teacher and spinster—the conviction that Fate had paid me the compliment of handing over the reins. She had failed to provide me that ideal relationship which alone is the basis of the true home, and I was by nature obdurate toward accepting anything less at her hands."

In 1912, taking advantage of the Enlarged Homestead Act which offered land primarily in the high desert, Alice Day, with the help of a "locator," settled on a 120-acre plot at the base of Friar Butte a few miles from Post, Oregon near the Maury Mountains. In 1914 she acquired a second plot. According to the Homestead Act, for each plot she had to put twenty acres under cultivation, which she did by herself, not to mention building her cabin, growing and harvesting crops, tending her chickens and cattle, and making ends meet by teaching in a nearby one-room schoolhouse—a ten-mile walk. She thrived on the challenges and developed a special affection for her barnyard friends. "A wholesome chicken yard, with its cackling, cawing, crowing, red-topped population...always greeting your coming with tumultuous welcome—it is a little nursery of pure joy in living, the epitome of ardent existence." She used her egg money to buy a horse. Fly, as she named him, made the plowing easier and provided a welcome alternative to walking the sixty miles to Prineville for needed supplies.

She was not afraid of hard work. To the contrary, she thrived on it. "Could I stack it (hay) alone? I confess it looked impossible. I could no less than begin, however, and begin I did. For one month, through long days of labor and nights devoid of ease...I tossed and tossed and stacked from morn to dewy eve. Nor was I in the end one whit the worse for the experience."

I was impressed. Could I work that hard? I remember so clearly, soon after I was married, when my husband made a trip to town, leaving me for the first time with a corral full of first-calf heifers. Heifers are cows that have never had calves. They sometimes have problems delivering the first time due to inexperience or, worse, due to the size of the bull they were bred to. My instructions as a newbie bride and rancher were to assist any heifer that had tried unsuccessfully to calve for over four or so hours. I was given two options.

I could do it myself. That involved coaxing the frantic and confused heifer into a stanchion in the barn, securing her there, reaching my rubber-gloved hand, sleeves rolled up to the elbow, inside her uterus despite her struggle and mooed protests, feeling around for and hopefully finding the feet of the unborn calf—unless it was breech, the head presenting first, in which case I would have to turn the calf around inside her, the strong sphincter muscle of the heifer closing like a vice around my arm. Once locating the soft hoofs I would secure the chain of the calf puller around them. (The puller is a primitive-looking implement that includes a breech spanner made of aluminum that goes across the heifer's rear end, a steel rod, a lever, and a chain.) Then I would winch the calf out of the mother in considerate rhythm with her contractions. Once the calf was delivered, I'd clean it off, then rub it roughly with hay to get its blood circulating, and finally stick a piece of straw up its nose to make it sneeze and breathe properly. The exhausted heifer (actually now officially a cow) still locked in the stanchion, I would hold the calf between my legs, next to the mother's udder, jam one of her teats in the calf's mouth and hope that her newborn would suck.

My second option was to chicken out and call the hired man.

When I did, my husband always let me know his disappointment. I had failed, once again, to "cowboy up," as he said. I managed some things on my own, some men's work. I harrowed, plowed, and swathed with the best of them, but always knowing, in case of a breakdown, I had a backup in the form of a him. When in charge of day-long cattle drives I nervously shouted myself hoarse issuing too many commands to the other wranglers, untethered and unconfident without the steadying presence of my spouse. I'd feign urgent domestic tasks on frigid winter mornings as my husband put on layers of clothing, felt-lined boots, and a scarf wrapped around his face to go feed cattle in blizzard conditions. You couldn't have paid me to offer to help him although sometimes, under the direst of circumstances, I had to. Some skills I was shamed into learning by other third- and fourth-generation ranch women. Without blinking they showed me how to castrate bull calves, tossing the testicles into a pail of water (and later preparing them as delicacies for dinner) while the bleating calf was held splayed on the ground between two taut ropes wielded by cowboys on horseback, or how to cruelly dig the beginning horn buds out of a calf's head with a sharp spoonlike instrument, to slice a wattle under the chin or on the flank with a knife, or how to jam needles into the infant hide or press the hot iron onto the flesh.

The thought of slaughtering my growing numbers of chickens appalled me until a neighbor, a third-generation ranch wife, came over and matter-of-factly guided me in equipping and readying the guillotine: buckets of boiling water, a chopping block, a sharp axe, and a coat hanger bent in the shape of a hook, attached to a broom handle. "Okay. Batter up," she said offhandedly. I gingerly snagged the foot of a chicken with the coat hanger contraption. Holding the bird upside down I topsied its small-brained universe completely, the confusion causing it to stop flapping its wings and hang limply from my hand. "Set it here." My neighbor gestured toward the chopping block as though indicating my place at a dining table. The head was on the ground in a second. I dropped the bird in shock and sure enough it ran around in decapitated, compass-less circles. They really do that. Though the quaint allusion doesn't mention the blood. "Running around like a chicken with its head cut off with blood gushing straight up into the air," would be more apt.

Grabbing the hapless bird I dunked it into the hot water, turning the liquid a murky rose color, then slapped the feathers off, the warmth dilating the skin's hold on the soggy, smelly, brick-red and white plumes. Soon it became rote, this process, a production line of ambush and slaughter and blood and feathers, both of us chatting away about trips to town, manicures, marriage. Once all the birds were slaughtered, I carried the stack of naked, newborn-sized bodies in my arms to the house for cleaning and final plucking until they looked ready for the oven. In my evolution, if you can call it that, as a ranch wife and ranch hand, in no time I would be offering my children the foot of a chicken I had slaughtered myself, a tendon or two sticking out for them to pull. It was one of their favorite pastimes.

A woman like Alice Day Pratt choosing to homestead alone was unheard of in these parts, in those times. A woman managing successfully on her own was threatening to the patriarchal system of ranching. Women were to be kept barefoot and pregnant, existed as a service organization to take orders from, support the activities and indulge the appetites of, their husbands. Alice Day paid dearly for her quiet, revolutionary ways. Mean-spirited and reactionary ranching neighbors took advantage of her property when she was away, turning their cows in on her fields and gardens. She was generally regarded with suspicion and as an oddity with the exception of the few bachelors in the area who viewed each and any schoolteacher as a possible wife. "One handsome Frenchman began at once in a businesslike way, spending Sunday afternoons with me. He brought, each time, a single vegetable as a present and as an example of his agriculture." But she avoided him. Despite all she was up against on her own, "the thought that spontaneity might become obligation was intolerable." She had reached the point that she "feared the lifelong bond."

Alice apparently recognized she had crossed some sort of emotional and personal continental divide and the momentum she was gathering coasting down the other side of Pike's Peak precluded, even trumped, certain options that might have been socially desirable to her before. The menopause of hope, of what's desired or, at this point, possible. Women's bodies offer all sorts of signs that things are stopping, changing. But linking the physical no-longer-possibles with diminishing social and professional options is slower to come. Pausing at the highest point on the see-saw, women are briefly afforded a view that reveals that even under the best of circumstances—good health, good luck—they don't have as long to live as they already have, possibly not even have half that much of quality time. And their options are narrowing. The cocoon and safety net of an intact marriage, family, and family traditions buffers this stare-down with mortality. But if the cocoon has been woven by you alone for any length of time, if catastrophe such as death of a spouse or divorce has left you solo, this can be a scary time. And sobering— for many women at this point acknowledge that having managed on their own, the idea of sharing their bed or life with someone is no longer a priority. But the related necessity to keep working and a solo old age lurks behind that decision. To paraphrase a poem by Oregon poet Marion Davidson:

the dream was only my own
and dinner was on my own.

I have arrived in this new land. I am single, middle-aged. I live within my means or try. I do and don't set my sights on finding a new partner. I love Dolly Parton's line from an early movie: "Don't know how many more fresh starts I got left in me." I am facing the possibility of life un-partnered until I die, hopefully a good twenty to thirty years from now. How can I make this an elegant exercise, not one that I, with some help from the culture I live in, regard as lesser, a failure to cowboy up to coupling?

In 1930, after eighteen years, Alice Day Pratt was driven out by drought and the ensuing Depression. She sold everything for what she paid for it and moved to New York City to live with her family where "sometimes, in the doubly walled shelter of a steam-heated apartment building I wake on a midwinter night and wonder whether the little house still stands in a wilderness of snow, and whether little calves are crying in the willows." She died in 1963 at the age of ninety-one.

## Alice DeLore (1908–2002)

Halloween was taken seriously by the ranchers who lived in the vicinity of the remote outpost of Paulina. Costumes were *de rigueur*. One year I borrowed a pair of my husband's coveralls, stuffed a small pillow under the bib, and donned an old man's rubber mask, which I crowned with a sweat-stained John Deere cap. The evening got off to its usual jaunty start, everyone arriving with potluck casseroles and desserts and lots of alcohol. The band was made up of various locals who could strum or sing or both. The selections favored "both kinds of music" as locals joked, "country *and* western." The tradition was that no one would reveal his or her true identity until midnight. It was surprising how few of my fellow ranchers I could identify, so diligent were they about remaining in character and so imaginative were their costumes. It turns out that the same was apparently true of my get-up. No one seemed to know who I was or, if he did, pretended he didn't. The women (I think they were women) danced with me in seductive fashion. Jolly Green Giants and Little Miss Muffets and robots in tinfoil-covered refrigerator boxes danced the night away.

Alice DeLore, happily ranching on her own on her isolated ranch since the death of her second husband Sedrick a decade before, arrived at the dance after things had been underway for awhile, her delicate and lean figure dressed not in costume but in her trademark blue jeans and a plaid shirt. She was known for her coquettish smile and love of dance and, some would add, flirtatious ways. I had seen her before at the small Paulina General Store where she did all her shopping. We'd nod a hello. That was the extent of it. However, on this night she studied me intently from the sidelines. She was probably in her early sixties, my age now, very attractive and surprisingly small, wrenlike, a startlingly small container for all the stories of living and running a ranch on her own.

Who knows what the truth was but the tales assumed a life of their own, some rivaling stories from the *National Enquirer* for their exaggerations and eccentricities: her first husband shot and killed

by a would-be suitor; she'd sooner walk to town than ride, sooner scale a fence than open a gate; her blood pressure medicine air-dropped by her neighbor each month and, in one especially severe blizzard, Alice lay down in her coveralls and made snow angels

Alice DeLore shows me her books

to signal her need for him to drop hay to feed her cows; no phone, no electricity, did her wash on a washboard and read by kerosene lanterns.

It was probably a little after 9 p.m. when she arrived at the dance. For the next three hours I was hounded by her, she apparently persuaded I was some new male talent she was not going to pass up. Maybe she took my mask for the real thing or just assumed only a man would dress up as a man or just wanted to call my bluff. Whatever her motive, she wanted to dance every dance with me. "That is my one thrill in life. I have always loved to dance," she was quoted as saying in the *Central Oregonian*. It was awkward, to say the least, and midnight came none too soon. When my identity was revealed, she was either so embarrassed by her advances, so pleased with her bluff, or so disappointed I wasn't her dream man, she left.

Looking for information on Alice DeLore I recently paid a visit to the Bowman Museum in Prineville—a gem of an historical museum. I scanned page after page of dog-eared scrapbooks molting old newspaper clippings, stumbling on a photo of a trim seventy-one year-old Alice DeLore as the fifty-third Pioneer Queen of Prineville in 1989. In the photo she is in a dress but her sprightly pose and purposefulness, her lean strength contradicts the frilly white frock. Ten years after that Pioneer Parade, she was quoted in the Prineville paper as saying: "Last time I saw my doctor about my high blood pressure, I told him, 'Well, I'm still livin' out there with my cows.' And he said, 'That's what is keepin' ya goin'!'" She reportedly wrote in a diary each evening about the weather, chores of the day, her thoughts. "I'm just livin' my life, goin' about my business like I have always done." "My philosophy is do the best you can day by day. Don't dwell on the past; think of tomorrow, and keep on goin'." "I'm so attached to this country and the quietness, and to lookin' after my cattle, that I don't ever want to leave or move away."

Every summer I lead a writing retreat in the high desert. The participants are lodged in a converted ranch house on land adjacent to Alice DeLore's old place. I visit her abandoned ranch each time, can almost feel her small, warm palm cup mine as I push the garden gate and let myself into her yard, now overgrown with tall rye grass. I picture her standing hunched over, blowing on the pilot light of her stove, pumping water, calling her chickens to roost. I once startled a wren nesting in the eave of the house. I was sure it was Alice.

The writers who attend the retreat take their turns, with their pads of paper and pens, drifting over the hill and along the dirt road riddled with badger holes that leads into Alice's place to deposit their big life questions on her altar. She would be amused, no doubt. She would carry on with whatever she was doing, wipe her hands on the ragged dish towel tucked into her belt, and head out to do a chore, throwing some words over her shoulder, like salt for good luck, about getting on with life.

There is a matrimony vine (*Lycium barbarum*) that still grows unchecked outside the kitchen window of Alice DeLore's ranch house, has spread up and over the remains of an arbor. It was said that women homesteaders welcomed something green in the dry desert and traditionally planted the tenacious vine, also known as the boxthorn, outside the kitchen for shade, handily positioned to receive the daily dousing of dishwater. Settler women passed on all sorts of medicinal claims about the licorice-tasting berries, including enhancing the immune system, improving eyesight and circulation, protecting the liver, and boosting sperm production.

Impressive, but I'm more interested in this vine that rails against the grey of life, gives some shade from the challenges, offers fruit that cures heartache. I will happily dance under its arbor and, inspired by you, Alice DeLore, twirl my can-do while I've got it. If some man out there wants to join in, well come on. Maybe I have another fresh start in me after all.

SOME OLD-TIMERS REMEMBER DAYS in the early 1900s when the sun was obscured by dust on the drive between Bend and Burns. It wasn't drought, not the high desert's version of the Dust Bowl; those roiling clouds of fine, chalky topsoil were caused by hundreds of horses on the move. "Along the highway a person could see five thousand at once," an old buckaroo once told me. "And every one of 'em belonged to Bill Brown." At that time it was said Bill Brown owned more horses than anyone on the Pacific Coast and possibly the United States. His Horseshoe Bar brand was blazoned on horseflesh running from Oregon's Fort Rock to Wagontire, from Gilchrist Valley to Alkali

Lake. No wonder he was proclaimed the "Range King," "King of the Desert." His ranch house and corrals were just over the hill from where my husband and I lived with our children and though he had died thirty-three years before we arrived on the desert, there were days when, heat dancing off the sage-covered hills, I swore I saw him walking the fence line.

If you're picturing John Wayne, if you're picturing a square-jawed, weather-beaten cowboy in leather chaps and silver-star spurs astride his high-stepping stallion, you're wrong. Bill Brown's six-foot frame was draped in oversized bib overalls, a worn vest, and a soiled white shirt. He wore lace-up, not cowboy, boots. In countenance he had more the air of a sharp-nosed preacher or mustached professor than a broncobuster. He was well educated, quirky, in some ways, genius. Reflecting on his college years at California State Normal School (class of 1878) Brown was quoted as saying: "I found I was deficient in classics. I was tough as whalebone, so I could put in twelve hours a day on my books. I would slip a Shakespeare or some other great writer into my pocket and, for exercise, take a four- or five-mile walk and by the time I was back to school I would have learned a page or two of worthwhile literature." He was trusting to a fault and assumed others to be as honest as he.

The expanses of the high desert suited this loner, also dubbed the "Horse King That Walked." It was ironic that, despite all the horses he owned, he only rode if there was no other option, preferring to go on foot, the ubiquitous book in his back pocket. Whistling to himself, he'd happily walk the desert for days. His ranch hands claimed he could outwalk any saddle horse. They also reported that though he had a size nine foot, he was said to always wear a twelve shoe and the rare times he did ride he'd take out his shoelaces so he could pull his feet free of the stirrups if his horse fell or bucked. Cowboys said on the rare occasions he rode, he would run his horse until it was completely winded and then get off and lead his mount twice the distance they had just covered at a gallop. More than likely it was Farewell, his loyal and long-suffering favorite mare, who tolerated this unusual treatment. A prophetic choice in name, for ultimately Bill Brown would be forced to say good-bye to his beloved desert and to his most cherished dreams. But there was no foreshadowing of that sad ending at the turn of the nineteenth century. This whistling, walkabout of a man seemed to have the Midas touch.

Bill Brown and two of his brothers got their start raising sheep in 1882 in Wagontire. After a series of severe winters that wiped out thousands of their sheep, his brothers had had enough and returned in 1890 to the Willamette Valley to farm. But Bill had found his soul's home and bought out their sheep and land holdings. By the 1920s he owned eight bands, three thousand per band, branded with the Horseshoe Bar on the nose and on the wool with a wooden "iron" dipped in red paint. If he found a herder lazy or wanting in some way or another, and he often did, Bill herded the sheep himself. "Herding sheep gives a man a lot of time for reading worthwhile books and doing worthwhile thinking." One herder recalls "Bill ... was with the sheep all the time." Another relates a time when Bill "canned every sheep herder he had. He moved over to Glass Buttes there at Browns Well and he had thirty thousand head of sheep he was herding himself." Many confirm he often trailed his bands the twenty miles from the Gap Ranch to Burns in one day and that he carried strychnine in one pocket to poison coyotes, and raisins or dried prunes in the other to provide him with some

Bill Brown

sustenance. Folks liked to tell stories about Bill getting the pockets mixed up or mixing the two in the same pocket. A good yarn, but just not so. Ingesting even a trace of strychnine would have killed him. At the height of his sheep years the bands ran from Wagontire to Buck Creek in southeast Crook County. He sheared the sheep at locations across his desert holdings and freighted the wool, four horses per wagon, all the way to The Dalles until 1910, when Oregon's first high desert railhead opened in Shaniko.

In 1903 the *Prineville Review* quaintly reported that five hundred of Bill's sheep were slaughtered by Paulina Sharpshooters using "the bullet method." But Brown suffered less than most during the range wars between sheep and cattlemen as he kept his bands off of what had been claimed as cattle country. On the public range he did use, he moved his herds from one allotment to another quickly so the land was never overgrazed. (It turns out that this rapid rotation approach to range management, now touted by university agricultural experiment stations as the way to protect native grass species, was pioneered in the high desert by Bill Brown.) The Range Wars subsided in 1906 when the United States government stepped in and allocated allotments specific to sheep and cattle on the unclaimed homestead offerings that were consolidated to form the Bureau of Land Management.

But never mind the welcome truce between cattle and sheep men. Never mind the ongoing profits he continued to make from selling his wool. Bill was already playing a new hunch. For years big cities across the United States had used draft horses to pull trolleys. When electricity was introduced in the 1890s hundreds of horses suddenly flooded the market. Bill bought all he could. Just because. Just because it seemed like a good idea. Just because he thought big and small at once. "Largely" as he put it. Just because he was "morally certain" there would be a use for them. "Half genius and half damn fool," was how he was described. How did he manage to think so big, living so small? How did he manage to imagine a future for those unwanted horses while walking the desert, herding sheep, a pocket full of raisins? There is something exquisite about the entrepreneurial mind, conjuring something out of nothing that spawns work, new ideas, material and financial rewards —unless, of course, the pursuit of those things is a compensation for something lacking in life.

In addition to the horses he purchased, he also had his cowboys chase down, corral, and brand as many of the horses they could find that ran wild in the high desert. They would use what is called a domesticated "prather" horse—also called a "Judas" horse—to trick and lead the wild horses into a corral. The wild ones were referred to as broomtails, fuzztails, or mustangs and some were said to be descendants of stock that arrived from Spain on the coast of Mexico with Cortez in 1514. Ranchers joked that these horses weren't wild at all, instead rodeo stock horses that didn't buck, so were turned out in the desert to fend for themselves.

But during a routine Bureau of Land Management roundup of wild horses in southeastern Oregon in 1977, a BLM employee noticed primitive marks on some, "resembling horses as they existed back to the Ice Age and to very high degree representing a type of horse brought to this country by the Spaniards." Subsequent tests showed this to be, in fact, true. Telltale is the dorsal stripe down the back ("linebacks") of the Kiger and the zebra stripes on their legs. The Kiger is small, fourteen hands or so, with hard feet and incredible physical endurance. Their coloring ranges from dun, claybank (white), darker brown, "grulla," or gray/brown to honey-colored. Horses segregate according to color. In addition the Kiger are known to scorn other

Wild Kiger mustangs

"wild" horses and have managed to keep the integrity of their breed intact although recently their numbers are being dangerously overwhelmed by other breeds turned out on the desert. The legendary stallion of the high desert's Kiger herd is "Mesteno" which means unclaimed horse in Spanish. Most Kigers trace their bloodlines to this one horse who lived his whole life on Steens Mountain. Today the Kigers are a tourist attraction. City slickers, or "goat ropers" as they are pejoratively referred to by cowboys, drive out into the high desert with their cameras poised to record a fleeting glimpse of the offspring of Mesteno. Every few years the wild herd is rounded up and the excess horses auctioned, an increasingly popular event. A record was set in 1999 when Steven Spielberg paid a reported $50,000 for a three-year-old stallion after which he modeled the movie *Spirit, Stallion of the Cimarron,* released three years later.

What with the horses purchased from across the United States, the wild horses he captured, and the horse trading he did in Oregon, by the early 1900s Bill had over seven thousand head that ranged across southeastern and central Oregon. When Brown bought out a rancher's herd, he "bought the iron," meaning that he bought every horse owned by the seller, giving Brown the right to that brand. The Running W on right stifle, BAR C on right shoulder, Bar Diamond on left—all were his.

His timing was uncanny. The year 1898 marked the war with Spain. Representatives of the United States Army cavalry traveled to Central Oregon to buy from Brown. Then came the Boer War (1899–1902) and Bill found a willing buyer in the English army. Eight years later, World War I created a demand, and he sold the horses he had bought at seven dollars for eighty-seven dollars. He auctioned his horses himself, seated on the top rung of his corrals at Lost Creek near Wagontire. The unwritten rule was if you purchased a Brown horse, the horse could not stay in the state of Oregon. Anything with the Horseshoe Bar brand in Oregon was assumed to be Brown's.

The buckaroos he hired to run the horses were closer to the John Wayne image of the American cowboy. The name, derived from *vacquero*, suggests the lineage of tradition these cowboys embraced and still do in their dress, language, customs, but most of all in their love of horses. Unlike their boss, they were happiest astride a horse. Search, capture, brand, broncobust. Their idea of heaven was "mare chasing." Eighty miles a day on horseback was nothing unusual. And then, as a way to relax, a buckaroo's idea of fun was described in this journal description by one of Brown's wranglers: "After a full day of riding (we trapped) five hundred in corral. Fifteen saddled up, ten bucked off."

Bill Brown finally settled on Buck Creek as his headquarters. Given all the picture-perfect valleys, seductive languishing draws he could choose from, why that location? His brilliance was not limited to sheep and horse markets. Bill Brown intuited that if he controlled the water, he controlled the high desert. Made sense, given the local anecdote: "Why, that time it rained forty days and forty nights, we got one inch and a half in the high desert." So what Brown bought were the locations that had water—springs, creeks. In those days Buck Creek ran year around. And there was lots of land for sale in the vicinity, and good grazing. He speculated the water could be moved to where it was needed and he was right. Bill Brown country is still laced with his handmade ditches, rock-lined aqueducts that hug the sides of hills and coolies and carried water to small fields and pasturelands. Said one: "Bill didn't need very many instruments. He had an awful eye, that old fellow."

A portion of the original house still stands, its white clapboards sidling up to the gentle willows of Buck Creek. It was said to be a replica of his brother's family home in Portland located on southwest Yamhill. Bill was one of seven children—all of whom did very well as doctors, farmers, community servants. Bill's father, a farmer himself, raised his children to work hard. His mother instructed them based on the teachings of the Bible. Bill was, needless to say, by far the most eccentric of his siblings. He did nothing halfway. I was reminded of that on a recent visit to what is left of the Buck Creek house. Taking in the classic and elegant structure I reflected on what an *Oregonian* reporter in 1915 was quoted as saying when he visited the brand-new house: "Splendid furniture, great ballroom, great baths, water system, living room, and Bill's office and bedroom combined. Fourteen rooms. Three bedrooms on ground, four more upstairs plus nursery." A ballroom? It was well known how much Bill liked to dance. He would host dances that lasted all night either in the largest room of his house, referred to as the ballroom, or the second floor of the Horseshoe Bar Store. People came horseback and in wagons, taking all day to get there. When the children got tired they would all be put in one big bed in the main house.

The Horseshoe Bar Store, which operated from 1910 until 1920, was torn down in 1942 and a garage now stands where it used to be. In its heyday it carried everything—food, hardware, tack, equipment parts. When Brown's wagons delivered wool to Shaniko, he'd have the drivers go on to The Dalles to pick up supplies for his store. He operated the store on the honor system, left it unlocked with a register for people to write down what they took, paid, still owed. "Most are honest. Some are not," Brown acknowledged. Later, slightly more chastened by experience, he would say, "I made a fortune, gave away a fortune, had a fortune stolen from me." Animals, equipment, and merchandise from his store and ranches were robbed. Bill refused to believe it. Once his sister had him confront a man she knew had stolen from him. Bill asked the man if he had. The man denied it. Bill turned to his sister and said, "See, what did I tell you. He's as honest as the day is new."

But who did he plan on dancing with, on partnering with? And why a nursery? As it turns out Bill Brown's most treasured dream was not money, thousands of sheep and horses, acres and acres of land—but a wife and children. "Shucks, confound it. I might just get married someday and if I do, I'll breed her in the fall and lamb her in the spring." He is said to have truly loved one woman, many years younger than he, and for whom he made a diamond studded locket in the shape of his famed Horseshoe brand. He paid her what would be his final visit, placing the chain around her neck and reputedly exclaiming; "Now I got my brand on you and you're mine." She was not impressed. She ripped the chain from her neck, threw the locket on the floor and stamped on it. After this heartbreak he saw women simply as a means to an end and tried crudely to persuade them to participate in his grand scheme. Despite being repeatedly rebuffed, even at fifty he still held out hopes for having "Seven sons on seven waterholes." "If I had sons I could own the whole state of Oregon."

Bill's approach was obviously not refined, not what the young women of the time were looking for. And some of his personal habits weren't either. According to Lena Wilson, who was his housekeeper starting in 1908, Bill was disinclined to bathe.

"Well, I am mighty certain I don't need it."

"Well, I'm mighty certain that you do. It has been over a week," Lena replied.

Lena recalls taking Bill by the hand and leading him to the bathtub and shoving him in. She did say, however, that he was always washed and clean for dances. His roughness distracted from the incredible integrity, imagination, and tenderheartedness of the man. Such was his reputation that the bank in Prineville honored checks with Bill Brown's signature presented on a board from the side of a homesteader's cabin, tomato soup can label, chip from a woodpile.

On my visit to the Buck Creek house, black wasps, clad in brittle tuxedos, made their buzzing home around an old ceiling light fixture in an upstairs bedroom. The telltale odor of packrats wafted through the living room. The paint on the exterior was all but gone. An elegant bay window looked uphill through the valley carved by Buck Creek. All the rooms had high ceilings, beautiful configuration. Narrow stairs led up to spacious bedrooms with large windows looking out over the narrow draw where the house sits flanked by poplars, across from where the Horseshoe Bar store used to sit. In the end only hired hands slept in the nursery until that wing of the house was torn down. The last dance was held in the store in 1935.

So, okay, a salty, intriguing desert character. A good read. But what else? Bill Brown realized some of his dreams, even some he didn't know he had. But he didn't realize what he most yearned for. Bill's singular focus on finding a wife and his conviction that all men are honest led to his demise. At what point does our focus on what we want become so singular that what we get is always found wanting? At what point does the insistence on a particular outcome obscure the life story that is trying to tell itself? To what extent should we focus and to what extent does focus prevent us from achieving our goals? They say to look to the left and the right of a star, not straight at it, to see the star more clearly. Bill Brown did that successfully with land and livestock. But when it came to matters of the heart and his assessment of others, he stared directly at the sun. How can we be light on our feet without being pushed over? How can we hold onto principles and goals without becoming inflexible? Is what we most want always what we won't get simply by virtue of the over-wanting? And what we do get is because accidentally we have not insisted? I'm inside these questions. They matter to me. I held on too long, too tight to my dream of raising a family on our high desert ranch. At this point I have held on too long, too tight to the story about the sad outcome.

With the advent of the automobile and the end of the war, Bill's horses were no longer needed. He stubbornly kept them in order to keep his ranch hands employed. By 1931 he was broke. He had watched his horses go for "chicken horses" to the packing plants in Portland—twenty-five hundred horses shipped per month for dog and chicken feed or for "pony coats," still popular at the turn of the nineteenth century. By 1935 everything he had worked for was no longer his. He was placed in an old persons domiciliary in Salem where he gave all the residents shovels and exhorted them to get out of their rockers and dig up the grounds for planting potatoes, all the while muttering his oft-repeated mantra: "Work hard from cradle to grave." He tried more than once to escape, to walk back to the desert from Salem, back to his beloved Buck Creek. In 1941 Bill Browne died in the Salem home at age eighty-five. One old Horseshoe Bar mare was last seen in 1953 somewhere near Gap Ranch, still roaming Bill Brown's range, its muzzle white from age. Maybe it was Farewell.

# Day in Court

LESS THAN OFTEN, MORE THAN ONCE, headed back out to our high desert ranch via Highway 20, I would be pulled over by the same state trooper. "You again," he would say. Humoring him, I'd point out that if he delayed me too long the ice cream would melt, gesturing toward the month's worth of groceries stacked high in the back of my station wagon; that husband and children were waiting and my babysitter probably worn to a frazzle. He'd usually wave me on good naturedly, but not before we took a moment to take in the eastern horizon basted in the rays of the sun setting behind us, behind the spires of the Cascade Mountains. He never wrote me a ticket.

The trip from the ranch to Prineville, Madras, Redmond, and Bend and back was a three-hundred-mile circle, took a full day. Tractor and swather parts, chicken feed, milk supplement, and veterinary medicine. I'd hurry through the smaller towns to make it on time for a late lunch with girlfriends in Bend followed by a quick game of tennis, outside if the weather was good, often at a friend's well-appointed ranchette, and if it was winter, in the Crane Shed, an old lumber storage building—an enormous basilica of a thing that had outlasted its usefulness and no longer stored cut lumber. Instead, someone with a sense and style of humor that seemed to be more prevalent in those days had installed a couple of makeshift tennis courts. If you put a quarter in the slot the lights would go on for an hour and, despite the dank cold and the pigeon poop, a decent game of tennis could be had. In 2007 the crumbling wooden structure became Bend's cause célèbre when a developer wanted to tear it down to make way for a new upscale mall. A protest was mounted and a plan to preserve the old crane shed as an historic building was presented to the City Council. But having calculated the worst-case fine he'd receive versus what his buyer would pay, the developer marshaled an army of gigantic front-end loaders and cats and knocked the shed down under the cloak of darkness before the City of Bend had come to any decision. The millions he received in the sale easily offset the paltry fine of $60,000 he was charged for his misdemeanor. The proposed development for the site has yet to materialize given economic downturns. The massive lot sits empty, affording an unobstructed view of the Deschutes River and the Cascades. Sagebrush and a few clutches of wild rye are starting to make a tentative comeback. Returned nesting ground sparrows quarrel over house sites.

Between trips to town I'd keep my tennis game sharp playing every once in awhile on the McCormack's tennis court at their ranch on Bear Creek. Cows would pause on their purposeless trips down the dirt road that flanked the court to apply their tiny brains to the question of why those humans were fenced inside such a small, grassless pasture. Coming up with no satisfactory answer, but no doubt pitying our lot, they moseyed away.

Sometimes I took my infant children with me on the runs to town, plopping them in a playpen in back of the station wagon, armed with zwiebacks. This was before the days of car seats and seat belts. They'd roll around inside, ricocheting off the padding, delighted with the turns. They'd chortle at the trooper when we were stopped. After taking in the sunset sometimes he and I would take a moment to compare our versions of life, love, and the pursuit. I saw only possibility, I told him. He waved me on home.

But today I was driving to Portland. I had by now lived in "town" for as long as I had lived on the ranch, my children grown and, for better or worse, on their own, their tormented father dead from a self-inflicted gunshot wound, my second marriage in a shambles, and I forcibly relieved of my naïve belief that things would turn out as I had hoped or dreamed: happy familial commotion, an enduring relationship, dare I say life on a ranch? On this trip I wasn't headed to town to buy farm implement parts. Instead I was driving from Bend to Portland and using that drive to put my parts back together, glad to think, reflect about the who, what, where, and why of my life that had played out on this high desert stage.

I drove through the Crooked River National Grasslands, a prairie that, as it approaches Madras, settles out into perfect fields of agricultural promise, giant pivots staggering like Frankensteins in stiff-legged circles. They irrigate rich harvests of mint, garlic, wheat, and seed crops planted right up to the front door of tidy, contrite farmhouses begrudgingly permitted a small corner of land next to looming machine sheds that shelter dinosaur-sized machinery. Madras is a microclimate, a farmer's heaven ever since a post-World War II project delivered water to its thirsty plains and long growing season. It is a town of unusual ethnic diversity: Native Americans thanks to the Warm Springs Reservation to the north, Mexicans thanks to the seasonal labor which spawned a permanent population, second and third generations of homesteading Caucasians. With its dry surrounds that encroach just beyond the irrigated fields; its low-slung, stucco buildings; its wide, dusty streets named after letters in the alphabet as though the town was to be only a temporary encampment, Madras has more the air of a sun-bleached southwestern border outpost than a town in the center of Oregon, an Oregon so often thought of (by those who don't know) as a state of lush green and endless rainfall.

But Oregon is, in fact, mostly desert. Oregon is mostly this gritty, beautiful, hardscrabble landscape. Madras in some ways most truly represents the region socially, economically, and environmentally. Its Central Oregon cousins seem to have taken on false identities

or lost them. Sisters pretends to be a western town with false fronts
and building codes that require that the ruse continue. Prineville,
once a mill town and a monument to the genius of Les Schwab,
who built his tire-manufacturing empire there, is now in search of
an economic identity since the closure of the mills, Schwab's death,
and the relocation of the headquarters. Bend seems preoccupied
with a more hip vision of itself, chasing a tourism-based economy
(dubbed "industrial tourism" by Edward Abbey) that is proving to be
as ephemeral as the morning dew. No, for a dose of what's left of the
real, go to Madras. I didn't anticipate what a bracing dose I would get.

I had just passed the auction yards coming off that straight stretch
of farmland. The yards are the last ones left in the region. It used to
be every town had its own. Redmond, in my lifetime, once had two.
At the Madras yards, the elevated boardwalks still crisscross above
pens filled with livestock. Buyers, in caps or cowboy hats, boots and
blue jeans, walk slowly back and forth like penitentiary guards as
though the cattle, horses, sheep, and pigs might be planning some
sort of insurrection. They hook their boot heels on the railing fence,
and pause long enough to hear the wind, to feel the dry heat, to smell
the fresh-cut alfalfa lying in windrows in the surrounding fields.
They write numbers down on the ubiquitous small spiral-bound pad
of paper carried in their ink-stained shirt pockets, and then lazily,
coolly head back into the auction barn. Inside the sawdust-covered
arena, the hazer on horseback herds the confused and scared animals
in frantic circles. The sing-song monotone of the auctioneer is spliced
with a loud "Hey!" or "Hut!" when he spots a bid signified by the
surreptitious touch of a cap brim, the tilt of a pencil, the lift of a chin.
"Sold!" And the reluctant performers are escorted abruptly off stage,
kicking their heels in protest against the nipping cow dogs.

Highway 97 is an interstate and yet is dangerously only two lanes
wide. Loaded cattle trucks swing wide to turn their big semi loads
slowly off the highway into the auction yards. School buses stop to let
off children. People drive all manner of rigs at all manner of speeds—a
plodding, extra-wide tractor going from one field to another; old

farmers in beat-up Chevy pickups in no hurry to get anywhere; reckless teenage drivers; migrant workers, ten plus, jammed into an overheated van, scarves hanging down from under their hats as if they were sheiks. The stretch of 97 between Bend and Madras is referred to as the ribbon of death, it has claimed so many lives. The highway jams together the pace of the country with the breakneck of getting somewhere fast, things to do on city time. I was on city time. Checking my watch, I realized I was running late. I stepped on it, sixty-five, seventy-five miles per hour, left the livestock auction in my dust. Then I noticed the flashing light in my rearview mirror. This trooper, unlike my friend from my ranching days, was in no mood for conversation. He cut me no slack. The hefty price tag on the ticket prompted me to decide to appear in court to see if I could get my fine reduced. On the appointed day I tiptoed slowly back to Madras, fifty miles per hour all the way.

At reduced speeds it's amazing what one sees. Red-tailed hawks diving for sage rats. The stooping ballet of the farm laborers, now out of their van, necks and faces covered, genuflecting toward the earth, a posture as old as time, memorialized on canvases across the world, symbolic of the relationship between landowners and their workers, gentry and peon. I saw horses startled by a dust devil, galloping, heads and tails high, across their pasture. I was struck by the perfection of the black Angus cattle against the green of the fields. Such a day! The sun sipped the moisture out of the ground through a straw, filled the air with smells of growing things.

The courthouse in Madras, constructed in the 1960s, is made of cement, solid, reinforcing the message of permanence and, in this case, the rule of law. On my scheduled day in court, and a few minutes late, I walked up the buffed linoleum steps, my hand gliding along a carved wooden banister. Large windows with vertical panes of glass framed the juniper-studded hills. The embedded perfume of years of Mr. Clean pinched the air.

I gave my name as I entered the room and took my seat in one of a row of oak pews separated by a wide aisle that led up to the thronelike chair of the judge. The court recorder sat at a table below on the right of the judge and on the left, one woman sat alone in the separate pews reserved for the jury. I didn't know her function and studied her for a clue. She was trim, short hair in tight round curls—Sunday morning Methodist curls. She wore a floral, belted dress, flat shoes, bifocals. She could have been seventy or even older. She sat schoolmarm straight, a pad of paper and pen in her lap. I still had no idea why she was there.

The judge was announced by the court reporter. "Please rise." All of us did. He ceremoniously entered the courtroom, throwing his long, black robes out behind him as he settled into his chair. In silence we, a motley crew of Mexicans, Native Americans, Caucasians, all sat back down. Already there was something otherworldly about this courtroom space and this appointed time.

There were nine of us scattered among the pews. Some mandated to appear, others like myself volunteering to do so, others there as support to their friends. As the last to arrive I would be the last to be called, so I sat and watched as each defendant walked down the aisle to stand before the judge.

When I was small, traveling by train in New England was common. My mother and I spent a lot of time in train stations going between our home in Andover ("And over, and over, and over!" the conductor used to call when we pulled into our station) and Boston, where most of her relatives—my aunts, uncles, cousins—lived. On those trips she introduced me to one of her favorite pastimes, inventing stories about the people waiting for the train. We sat next to each other on the wooden bench whispering our invented histories about the man with the cane, the young mother and her fussy baby. I still survive long airport delays with this distraction and in the Madras courthouse on this day I had plenty of fodder, and time, as I awaited my turn.

Across the aisle from me was a picture-perfect young teenage couple. Their fingers twined and untwined, their thighs pressed against each other's, her head against his chest—as many body parts touching as was publically acceptable. He wore jeans that traced his muscled thighs, his manhood. A cotton shirt hung loosely off his shoulders. She was sheathed in tight pants, her perky ripeness contained inside a halter top, her eyelids painted bright blue, and a fountain of blonde hair twisted into a barrette and pinned at the back of her head.

When he was called and got up to walk toward the judge, she leaned forward desperately as though unable to breathe without him. She gripped the edge of the pew, watched intently as he strode toward the judge, pulling his cap off his head at the curt instruction of the court reporter. He stood upright before the judge, yes sir, no sir, maintained he had been falsely accused by the police officer, that the report indicates a collision and there was none, instead his empty gooseneck horse trailer had hit some gravel on a turn and fishtailed but he was driving under the speed limit. His girlfriend silently mouthed every word he said, inching her way along the pew closer to the aisle, closer to him. No other vehicles were involved and he did not hit the guardrail. The officer had accused him of things he did not do. Farm kid, I thought. White bread. Entitlement. Marry young, maybe the girl he was with, carry on farming the land his father farmed, his grandfather farmed. He'd been driving tractors and balers since he was ten. Knew seasons. Knew the hardship of losing a calf, a crop. Men had their job: work hard, play hard. Women had theirs, supporting their husbands. Life was black and white, in bold letters, easy to read and understand. In keeping with happy endings the judge dismissed the case. The boy sauntered back to his pew, gestured to his girl, and the two walked out side by side. He playfully hooked his fingers in the belt loops of her tight jeans, pulling up on them slightly. She laughed.

Next, a young Native American woman, maybe five feet tall, stocky, joined by two white girls there to support her. Lots of whispering and commotion among them. She giggled after every answer to the judge. Like a teenager. Only she wasn't and it wasn't her first offense and she had not paid a previous traffic violation. The judge levied a high fine and a stern warning. She and her friends left, noisily reasserting their version of the story and of the world. But the reality of the decision that day would catch up with her. I could see it. Her version of the world would not stand a chance. She was naïve and vulnerable and she was asking and relying on directions from people as lost as she.

Come To The Meet Market! was embroidered in red letters across the back of her shiny, purple jacket, part of "Meet" covered by the stringy, blonde ponytail of the next woman called to the bar. The smell of cigarette smoke followed her up the aisle. The judge addressed this rough-hewn woman in a weary, familiar tone, asked her why she was again driving with a suspended license, had failed to take care of other misdemeanors. Was she aware this behavior would land her in jail?

"I drove cuz no way else to get to work. Ain't gonna hitch, ain't gonna walk I'll tell you what. Not all the way from the rez." The judge and his threats didn't worry her. She had twenty-four hours to come up with the money for the past tickets? What a joke.

"I don't got that kind of money."

"The court can assist you with a payment schedule."

Her body language made it clear that the possible repercussions were nothing compared to what she confronted at home with her husband who sat in the courtroom, his belly resting on his knees, his thick, brown arm slung over the back of the pew, nothing compared to life on the reservation as a white woman.

There was one more to be called before it was my turn. His dark pants were pressed, his white shirt clean, a crucifix around his neck. His dark hair was slicked and neat, some grey appearing above his ears. He wore boots, the heels worn so far down on the outside his knees splayed slightly. The elderly woman with the gray pin curls, who had sat through the proceedings, now got up and stood by the defendant in front of the judge. Why? I wondered. He turned his cap in his hands, stood head down before the judge as though he had entered church.

He had. At least that's how my invented story about him went. His future was in the hands of this priestlike figure seated up above him. He was used to bowing to authority, to work in the fields. He wanted to believe in this system, any system, just as he wanted to believe in God. That the right thing, the just thing can happen. Will happen. That he will experience it before his time is up. That he is seen, recognized by powers greater than himself. Maybe he would find a place that received him, absolved him of his troubles, soothed his brow, held him, recognized him for the honest and hardworking man he was. No *mordida*. No graft. No hardship. No unfairness. Things would fall into place. All that had gone before would now make sense— leaving Mexico, getting his papers, years of farm labor in California and now in Oregon. That his wife would get the medicine she needed for her diabetes. That he could afford false teeth. That his children and grandchildren would uphold the values he stood for. That the droopy pants, tattoos, chains, and backward caps of his grandsons meant nothing, were just a style, a phase. This courtroom, salvation. This churchlike space, redemption.

When the judge asked for the defendant's name, the elderly woman by his side effortlessly and instantaneously translated what the judge said into Spanish and then what the defendant said into English. She is the court translator? I don't know what I thought one would look like, but this apple-crisp woman was not it. She repeated in perfect Spanish without inflection or emotion the judge's observations that all the required documents from his years working in California had been submitted, showed no infractions, that, on review, he was properly licensed. The judge paused and reflected for a moment, leafing through the papers. The only sound in the room was that of the judge tapping the end of his pen on his desk. He leaned back in his swivel chair, looked directly at the man before him. "Case dismissed." The Mexican man did not move. The translator repeated what the judge had said. "Case dismissed."

The man, his cap in his hands held against his waist, respectfully bowed his head. "*Gracias.*"

I couldn't restrain myself. I yelled out "Bravo!" as he walked out of the courtroom. My faith in the order of things, the possibility of happy outcomes, not just for the entitled but for Everyman, had been restored; the perfection of life's theater, the cautionary tales and parables every moment affords. "Order in the court!" reprimanded the judge. "Next defendant: Ellen Waterston. Please approach the bench." My fine was reduced. I drove back to Bend slowly, much more slowly, and richer, far richer.

# Upper Country News

I AM IN SITKA, ALASKA. I AM HERE on a writing residency, the guest of the Island Institute. It is early April. The shores are milky from the milt of herring. Tiny pearls of translucent roe coat the flat, brown tongues of ribbon kelp. The day I arrived, the purse seiners charged and wheeled their million-dollar boats in the shallow waters, jockeying to set their nets just right, scoring shocking numbers of herring when they did. Their language: gangions, longlines, jigs, and power blocks. Their prey: rockfish and sablefish, salmon and herring. Their competition: sperm whales and sea lions, sports fishermen and trawlers. Their wisdom keepers: the Tlingit Indians.

There are fourteen miles of road, eight thousand people, and a thousand grizzlies on this island. The local Raven Radio announces brown bear sightings as matter-of-factly as teen poetry night, pilates classes, or a potluck celebrating the local high schooler who won the Alaska Airlines drawing contest. Her design will adorn the tail of a plane that flies people up and away from this scythe-shaped Sitka in the archipelago of southeastern Alaska. She is a local legend now. Hannah Hamburg. The young girls of the island chant her name as though by doing so they will breathe her good fortune into their futures. Hannah, Hannah, Hannah.

For millennia the Tlingit people have breathed their chants and stories across Sitka Sound's islands and waters. Legends that explain catastrophic natural occurrences, songs that bring the salmon home, stories that mourn the loss of a village, the disappearance of a food source. Generations of Natives have fished here. Over time the white man moved in to claim the abundance of the seas for himself. Greed, scarcity, wasting turn out to be white man's diseases. Trickster ravens barking and gargling from the trees confirm it is so. Bald eagles, common as seagulls, whistle their shrill concern.

This place rains and drips and oozes stories. Watery stories. Ocean stories. And not just Native stories. Seated in warm kitchens, nibbling poppet beads of roe off seaweed as deftly as the sperm whale has learned to slip the black cod off the long liner's hook, swallowing thin leaves of smoked salmon with as much pleasure as the sea lion gobbles the whole fish, I have listened to stories of adventures from third- and fourth-generation fishermen. Their boats are tightly moored in the harbor, their small houses huddled against the slope of the mountains like a litter of mongrel pups. The looming peaks seem to have had enough of the lot of them, would just as soon push them into the ocean and reclaim their ground.

The Tlingit would agree about the unkindly motives of the mountains. Their legends cast the peaks, in their cape of clouds, as the symbol of the dark side—inscrutable, impenetrable, the source of bad things. A man's head crushed between the hulls of two boats. The battered women housed at the shelter. Two orphaned brown bears kept inside the walls of the closed pulp mill's slurry tank. Visitors pay to see the animals wandering hopelessly among a pile of discarded refrigerators, a big mud puddle in the middle of the round fortress. Blame the mountain spirits.

If the steep, tree-covered black mountains represent evil for the Tlingit, the ocean is the canvas for the dance of light, the source of good things, a world where the storms of life can be spotted a long way off. My first night here I heard *Yaaw Tei Yi*, the herring rock song, drummed and sung by a Tlingit woman. It tells the story of a year the herring were late. Would they come at all? A Native girl sits on a rock in the water and sings to the herring. She is chided by her clan for being lazy, for not helping with preparations for the return of the fish. She sings and sings, sings herself to sleep, her long black hair drifting out across the surface of the water. When she wakes, her hair is filled with herring eggs. Now every year the herring rock song is sung. And the herring come. The commercial fishermen feel better about their chances, knowing the herring rock song has been sung, though they wouldn't admit it.

I have worked on a number of projects at the Confederated Tribes of Warm Springs, an hour's drive from Bend. Three tribes share the same reservation lands: Warm Springs, Wasco, both formerly Columbia River tribes, and Paiute, a nomadic, high desert tribe. As a result of that experience, I am completely persuaded of the power of the tribes' mystical practices and beliefs. I witnessed a chief sing the eagle song to the dawn—the sun, on cue, breaking through the clouds to light up his face. I listened to the hypnotic cadence of the Native drumming and chants, moved by the energy and spirit of tongues I couldn't understand. Had I not had reason to spend time there, I would not have experienced the Native traditions I was allowed to observe. The Native culture of Central Oregon is not accessible unless you go to the reservation where Native and non-Native look at each other with suspicion, where the white man feels a trespasser and the Native a cultural prisoner. Reservation-bound tribes are ghettoized, treated as a sideshow, something on display at All Indian Days rodeos or dedications of institutions that include beadwork or basketry. But in Sitka, the Natives, their culture, and their stories are incorporated into the community. Here, the Tlingit define this island, as much if not more than any subsequent settlers. Their beliefs and reverence for the natural world in some ways serve as a needed drag anchor on the white man's hasty and intemperate ways.

I am from a storyteller tribe. My father handed the tradition to me as a child every night at bedtime, delighting me with his invented stories. My favorite was about a woman who played the piano with her toes. He never said: "You can do anything regardless of the challenges." He didn't have to. The story did. Or the duck that paddles in milk until it turned to cream. He never said: "Hard work will get you where you want to go." My mother too, with her railroad station game, conjuring tales about the others in the station waiting room. Not to mention her endless supply of stories about relatives and friends. On my own, the woods and the ponds of my New England childhood entranced me, elf villages secluded under moss-covered branches. The tide pools of Buzzards Bay became tiny harbors of my imagination where mussel shell boats were moored.

Shoving early poems and short stories into a drawer, I molded my own storytelling instincts into journalism—a college newspaper, as campus stringer for *Time* magazine, and later, on the staff of magazines based in Boston and New York City. Most recently I was the launching editor of a slick Bend lifestyle magazine. But my favorite journalistic stint was with Prineville's bi-weekly, the *Central Oregonian*, as the writer of the Upper Country News. The upper country took in such urban centers as Izee (named after the IZ brand and once a small mill site though nothing's left of it now) and Suplee (not much there either), as well as Paulina and Post. I eventually expanded my beat to include Brothers on Highway 20 and the Lone Pine Valley near Prineville. The column had traditionally served to inform upper country residents of who had attended which social gatherings, cribbage games, dances, and potlucks in an unembellished fashion. But I seized on the excuse to hide behind the role of reporter while I studied and learned about a lifestyle new to me.

I encountered all kinds in my upper country travels: the hired man who'd sneeze from the moment he got up until he put his socks on; Willard Powell, the rancher with two cowboy hats, one a go-to-town grey felt Stetson and the other a battered straw work hat. His cow dog knew that only the work hat was an invitation to go along. The rancher would demonstrate his dog's intelligence by taking one hat off and putting the other on in rapid succession, prompting such manic swings in the dog as to seem cruel.

*Upper Country News* documented all the rural ranching ways to have fun. Spring and summer evening jackpot steer ropings at one ranch or another, everyone's infants stuck in the same playpen, out of harm's way while their parents took turns chasing after a steer, one heading, throwing a rope around the horns, the other heeling, trying to snag both feet. Everyone threw in a dollar per round, the winning team splitting the take. Beer, lots of it, and the proverbial salads and casseroles served on tailgates fueled the festivities until darkness closed down the fun. The annual turkey shoot. Roast a pig in a pit. Organize rounds of skeet. Winners take home a frozen turkey. Townspeople invited. One woman from Bend, who had never held a gun, the butt gingerly pressed against her shoulder, gamely yelled "Pull!" Instead of launching a clay pigeon into the air, the skeet shooter, my husband, threw up his hat. She blasted it. Or how about the spring softball tourney in a hay field, meadow muffins as bases? Roy never did think to pull up his pants when he came to bat despite the chants: "Roy's up at bat, by cracky!"

Interviewing Willard Powell

I recorded extreme weather conditions not of interest anywhere else. South Fork of the Crooked River and Camp Creek flooding so much that ranchers motored through their fields in their aluminum skiffs. Determined to make it to her baby's shower in Paulina, one mother, clutching her swaddled infant, traversed two flooded rivers in the buckets of two different backhoes, met on either side by waiting ranchers who ferried her to the next fording. The deep freeze that froze chickens to their roosts, killing them. The party lines jammed with jokes about which ranchers' cocks froze overnight.

I didn't realize it, but as I recounted these anecdotes, I was bearing witness to traditions and a way of life that were vanishing due, primarily, to emerging new economic realities. Increasingly small-scale ranching didn't pencil. The sale of owner-operated ranches meant fewer resident families, which meant fewer children of school age—a death blow to many rural schools. Schools that provided reasons for the community to gather. Talent shows, fundraising bazaars to subsidize field trips, holiday pageants, graduations, and field days that gave the community something to cheer about. The minute children were bused long distances to schools in town, or sent to board with friends or relatives, or relocated to town with their mothers, a cornerstone was pulled from the arch of the rural community. Parents could forget the importance of their involvement in their children's education and with each other. Communities could forget what it was to gather, could forget their stories.

Every day, headed to the two-room Lone Pine School, the school bus used to cross the Crooked River on a one-lane wooden bridge and every day, just as it did, the children on the bus would lift their feet up off the floor, try to touch the ceiling with one hand, and chant "The ghost train!" pointing with their other at a railroad crossing sign teetering high above on the edge of a cliff. Time and again the bus driver would tell the story of the ghost train that traveled through the sky at night when all children were asleep. If they had been good, they weren't carried off by the train. If they hadn't, well… Their noses pressed to the windows, their necks craning to catch a last glimpse of the sign, in rapt silence they imagined the train rushing through the star-studded high desert night sky.

Paulina's elementary school has valiantly managed to keep its school doors open in the face of lower enrollment. The Brothers and Lone Pine schools have closed. The ghost train doesn't pass through anymore, not without a storyteller, not without someone to listen.

These stories are the daily bread of our communities, make up our cultural mythology. In communities like Bend that have experienced rapid growth and an influx of new residents, such stories and the cultural context they provide are lost, marginalized, locked up in historical societies or museums. In a culture that extols youth, who needs these stories, who'd hang around someone old enough to know them, who would want to? What happens, then, is the cultural landscape is replaced with a mono-story, a non-story. A non-story because it loops back on itself, is its own context. If you listen, the Central Oregon ponderosa forests still breathe Native songs. The songs of the logger still echo in the woods. The voices of buckaroos and homesteaders still whisper through the sage.

This is not news. If you don't learn from the past, which is to say hold your story, your community's, your state's, your nation's up against many stories, history is guaranteed to repeat itself. This is true in the broadest sense but also, personally.

I have spent a long time absorbed in my own story, turning the pages of my past over and over again, searching its chapters for something I missed, something that would change its outcome, would conjure a loving father and husband, resurrect our ranch life together, undo the hurts to my children, remove the sting of heartbreak. I'd pass my self-created roadside shrines gaudily decorated with plastic flowers, each a tacky monument marking the head-on with my husband's addictions, sideswiped guilt and regret, falling asleep at the wheel of my dreams. I was blind to the new story that I was living into, deaf to the rich landscape of others' stories that would inform mine, dumb and dumber in my myopia. The mono-story had me. I was a prisoner.

I had begun noticing I felt bigger, more possible when I spent time out in the high desert. But one day, driving back to Bend, I felt like the amazing shrinking woman. I decided it was the crush of my history in this place. I wondered if I would have to leave to get out from under the tyranny of this feeling. Maybe my time in the high desert had come to an end. Maybe the place I thought was home had betrayed me. Maybe I was lost here, lost to myself.

During my stay in Sitka I attended a ceremony to reclaim from "the dark side" a park where many women had been assaulted at night. We gathered for drumming and singing. We crafted luminaries by decorating and painting white paper bags, weighing them down with sand, and placing a lit votive candle inside. We made our way in the pitch dark to position them where women had been attacked, one murdered. It was hard to see, to find our way. I tripped on tree stumps, got snagged by branches. Massive Tlingit totem poles with stylized carvings of eagle, frog, and salmon brooded over our ritual. We walked in silence. Then one woman, a survivor, broke the quiet. She asked us: "Does anyone want to see where I was found?

The process of assembling the homespun desert wisdom in these essays has put on the page what is so grounding, so essential about the landscape of the desert and its people. It's the "dead as a nit," "sorry about your luck," "hard as a picnic egg," "make a hand," "cowboy up," "keep a deep seat loose rein" approach to things. My past is exactly where it belongs. Behind me. I was a prisoner inside my own story. Wishing certain things didn't happen is like wishing Rapunzel short hair or Red Riding Hood no grandmother. Hobbling the new story that is unfolding with wishes or regrets prevents living life fully. Turns out I wasn't lost in the high desert, but found.

Ellen Waterston is the author of a verse novel, *Vía Láctea: A Woman of a Certain Age Walks the Camino*, published in 2013 by Atelier 6000 and subsequently produced as an opera in 2016. Her two collections of poetry, *Between Desert Seasons, Poems* and *I Am Madagascar*, each won the WILLA Award in 2009 and 2005 respectively. Her memoir *Then There Was No Mountain* was selected by the *Oregonian* as one of the top ten books in 2003 and was a finalist for *Foreword*'s Book of the Year Award. She founded and, for twelve years, directed The Nature of Words. She is president of the Writing Ranch (www.writingranch.com) and founder of the Waterston Desert Writing Prize. After two decades of ranching Waterston is now based in Bend, Oregon.